"Book Publishing Blueprint:
How To Self Publish & Market
Your Books...Fast!"

By

Kent Mauresmo
Anastasiya Petrova

Copyright

Legal Terms

Disclaimer & Terms Of Use

The information contained in this material (including, but not limited to any manuals, CDs, recordings, MP3s or other content in any format) is based on sources and information reasonably believed to be accurate as of the time it was recorded or created. However, this material deals with topics that are constantly changing and are subject to ongoing changes RELATED TO TECHNOLOGY AND THE MARKETPLACE AS WELL AS LEGAL AND RELATED COMPLIANCE ISSUES. Therefore, the completeness and current accuracy of the materials cannot be guaranteed. These materials do not constitute legal, compliance, financial, tax, accounting, or related advice.

The end user of this information should therefore use the contents of this program and the materials as a general guideline and not as the ultimate source of current information and when appropriate the user should consult their own legal, accounting or other advisors.

Any case studies, examples, illustrations are not intended to guarantee, or to imply that the user will achieve similar results. In fact, your results may vary significantly and factors such as your market, personal effort and many other circumstances may and will cause results to vary.

THE INFORMATION PROVIDED IN THIS PRODUCT IS SOLD AND PROVIDED ON AN „AS IS" BASIS WITHOUT ANY EXPRESS OR IMPLIED WARRANTIES, OF ANY KIND WHETHER WARRANTIES FOR A PARTICULAR PURPOSE OR OTHER WARRANTY except as may be specifically set forth in the materials or in the site. IN PARTICULAR, THE SELLER OF THE PRODUCT AND MATERIALS DOES NOT WARRANT THAT ANY OF THE INFORMATION WILL PRODUCE A PARTICULAR ECONOMIC RESULT OR THAT IT WILL BE SUCCESSFUL IN CREATING PARTICULAR MARKETING OR SALES RESULTS. THOSE RESULTS ARE YOUR RESPONSIBILITY AS THE END USER OF THE PRODUCT. IN PARTICULAR, SELLER SHALL NOT BE LIABLE TO USER OR ANY OTHER PARTY FOR ANY DAMAGES, OR COSTS, OF ANY CHARACTER INCLUDING BUT NOT LIMITED TO DIRECT OR INDIRECT, CONSEQUENTIAL, SPECIAL, INCIDENTAL, OR OTHER COSTS OR DAMAGES, IN EXCESS OF THE PURCHASE PRICE OF THE PRODUCT OR SERVICES. THESE LIMITATIONS MAY BE AFFECTED BY THE LAWS OF PARTICULAR STATES AND JURISDICTIONS AND AS SUCH MAY BE APPLIED IN A DIFFERENT MANNER TO A PARTICULAR USER.

Contents

"Do you want the PDF Version of this Book?"

At the end of this book, I've included a link so can
download the full color PDF version for Free.

Quick Introduction

I know introductions are boring, so I'll make this quick! My name is Kent Mauresmo and I'm one of the bloggers at http://read2learn.net. I'm also one the authors of the kindle eBook, "**How to Build a Website with WordPress...Fast!**" and "**SEO For WordPress: Beginners Guide.**"

The main reason I'm writing this book is because the other books I read on this subject weren't that good. For example, I was reading an eBook that said, "*If you want to create a winning eBook cover, look at the Top 100 best sellers on Amazon Kindle and copy their book cover ideas.*" I think that's a bad idea for 3 reasons:

1. Most the book covers in the Top 100 are not that attractive.
2. As an indie author, you want to <u>stand out as unique</u>, not blend in with the crowd.
3. A lot of the authors in the Top 100 are well known, famous, and repeated **New York Times Bestsellers**. It doesn't matter what their book covers look like because their books are going to sell.

You need to be unique and create your own **fans**. If you try to copy somebody else, you'll just come off as a cheap knock-off. You need to stand out and <u>rise</u> above the noise.

<u>Disclaimer:</u> This book may have some flaws and maybe a few grammatical errors. If you read for style, or for literary quality, then this probably isn't the book for you. The only objective of this book is to show you:

1. How to create engaging book titles.
2. How to create your own unique book covers. (Winning color combinations)
3. How to **get your book formatted** for Amazon Kindle. (Outsource)
4. The right way to publish on Amazon Kindle.
5. Why I recommend enrolling into the Kindle Select Program.
6. How to set up an engaging <u>Amazon Central Author</u> profile.
7. How to get "**Amazon Verified Purchase**" reviews the easy way.
8. How and where to upload samples of your new book.
9. Most importantly, how to **build an online presence** and promote your book.

Some of the ideas presented in this book might be old, but some of them might be new. Either way, I'm not going to just tell you what to do, I'm going to actually <u>show you</u> with screenshots.

If the screenshots are too small to read, just download the PDF version of the book because the screenshots are a lot bigger. If you're ready, then let's get started!

Chapter 1.

How to Create Engaging Book Titles (Fiction)

If you're a fiction writer, you need to create book titles that make your readers ask questions. This is actually a good time to look through Amazon's Bestsellers list to see which book titles catch your attention.

I just looked myself, and I'm going to tell you which book titles caught my eye and why. Keep in mind that I don't read fiction books, so my opinion is completely unbiased. Here's a book that caught my attention:

Figure 1

This is a book by Gregg Hurwitz called, "*They're Watching.*" (*Figure 1.*) I'm not familiar with Gregg Hurwitz, but **his book title is engaging**. It makes me ask myself questions such as:

1. Who's watching?
2. Why are they watching?
3. Is this book about stalkers?

The title of his book is **mysterious**, and I want to "click" on it to find out more. Here's another book that caught my eye:

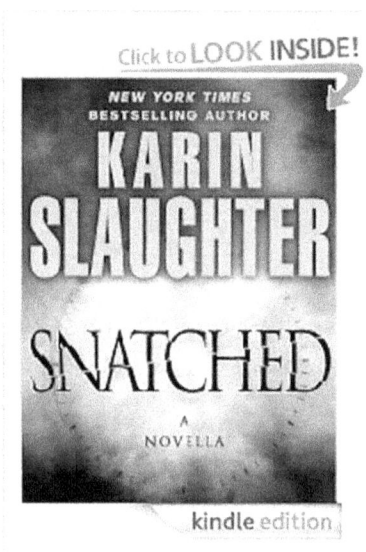

Figure 2

This book called "*Snatched*" by Karin Slaughter caught my attention because it makes me wonder **who's been snatched**. (*Figure 2.*) Did a kid get snatched? Was it an adult? Why were they snatched? Also, why is the author's last name **Slaughter**?! That's an excellent last name, I love it! I'll talk more about pen-names later.

Here's one more example that caught my attention:

Figure 3

"Dark Places" by Gillian Flynn has a simple title, but it's <u>very engaging</u> at the same time. (*Figure 3.*) By just looking at the title, do you know what this book is about? I don't! The title of this book makes me want to buy it because, once again, it seems **very mysterious**.

Short abstract titles seem to work very well for fiction authors. You have the <u>peak your reader's interest</u> so they'll click on your book to find out more.

Now here's an example of a book title that I *personally* think is not that good:

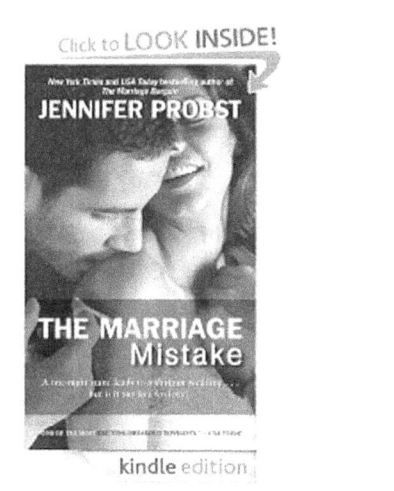
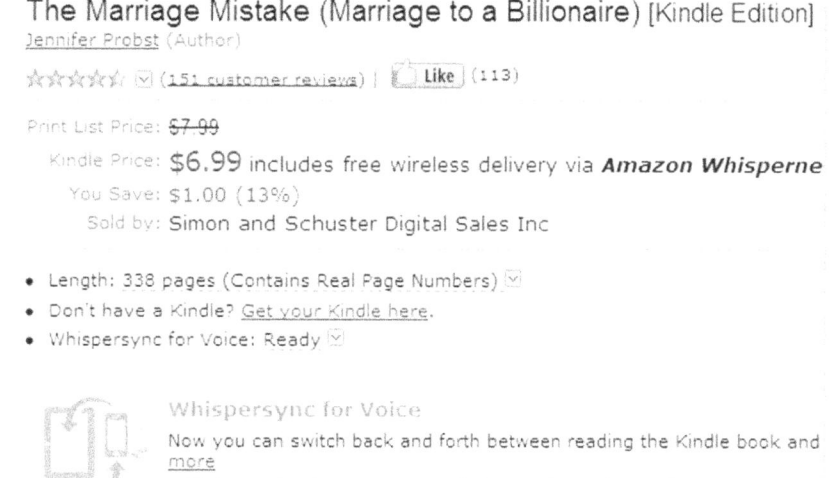

Figure 4

This book by Jennifer Probst didn't leave anything to my imagination. (*Figure 4.*) If the book was just titled, *"The Marriage Mistake"* then I would have wondered what it's about. Instead, the author has added to the title by saying *"Marriage to a Billionaire"* which gives it away for me.

Keep in mind that this is just **my opinion**. This author's book ranks in the <u>Top 10</u> as I write this, so obviously she knows what she's doing. It's also important to note that if *Jennifer Probst* ranks in the Top 10, then I highly doubt she's an Indie author.

So based on these examples, it's good to keep your fiction titles **short**, **abstract**, and **mysterious**. If a potential reader wants to know more about your book, they can click on your title and read the description.

For example, *"The Hunger Games"* is a really good book title. You'd have no idea what *The Hunger Games* is about by just reading the title. Abstract titles like that work very well for fiction books <u>only</u>! I don't recommend using this same technique for non-fiction books.

How to Create Engaging Book Titles (Non-Fiction)

If you write non-fiction books like myself, then your book titles **should not** be abstract or mysterious. Your book title should let potential readers know **exactly** what your book is about.

A lot of non-fiction authors try to come up with <u>clever titles</u> because they think it's cool. Guess what? It's not cool. If someone wants to learn *how to build a website*, how do you think they will search for a book on Amazon? They will most likely type, "how to build a website" into the Amazon search box right? So here are 3 examples of **good book titles**:

1. "How to Build a Website Fast"
2. "How to Create a Professional Website"
3. "How to Easily Build a Website: Beginners Guide"

Those are excellent book titles because they are <u>direct</u> and to the point. You'll also increase the chance of your book showing up on the first page of Amazon for the search term "*how to build a website.*" Now here are a few examples of **bad book titles** on the same subject:

1. "Website Delight: As Easy as 1-2-3"
2. "Under Construction: Website Guide"
3. 'Website Domination – The Ultimate Tutorial"

Some people reading this book might think those titles are cool and interesting, but they're not. Those book titles don't make any sense. The last book title, "*Website Domination-The Ultimate Tutorial*", is the **worst** of them all for 2 reasons:

1. By reading that title, you wouldn't know that it's a book about building websites.
2. The title makes a claim that it's "The ***Ultimate*** Tutorial."

The quickest way to get bad reviews is to claim that your book is the ***Ultimate*** Guide, the ***Best***, or has some "***top secrets***" that no one else knows about. You'll just attract readers that are already knowledgeable in your subject which isn't good. If they read your book and don't learn anything new, then get ready for a 1 star rating and a review that reads something like:

"*I wouldn't call this the ULTIMATE guide as the author claims. Most of the information in this book is outdated and can be found for free on Google. If you're a complete newbie then you might find 1 or 2 helpful tips, but I wouldn't recommend this book. This was a really quick read and I didn't learn anything that I didn't already know.*" – **Mr. Disappointed** ☹

It's always better to under-promise and over deliver. You want to <u>exceed expectations</u>. Even if you think your book is the *ultimate* guide, just call it a "**beginner's guide**" instead. Now after someone reads your book they'll think, "*Wow! That book had a lot more information that I expected! 5 STARS!!* ☺"

Looking through Amazon, here are a few examples of **good non-fiction book titles**:

Figure 5

This book entitled "*Home Cleaning Shortcuts*" by Heather Lane is direct and to the point. (*Figure 5.*) You know exactly what this book is about just by reading the title. Excellent!

Here's another good book title:

Figure 6

This salad recipe book is the best example by far! (*Figure 6.*) The book title implies that all the recipes are **easy**, you'll **impress your family**, and it's a **step by step guide** with **pictures**! To top it off, the author uses the last name "*Cooker.*" That's a nice Pen-name to use for recipe books.

Now here's an example of a <u>bad</u> book title:

Figure 7

"*A Little Bit of Everything For Dummies*"..?? That's not a good book title at all. (*Figure 7.*) I actually downloaded this book just because it was free. Several months have passed, and I still haven't opened this book because I don't know what it's about.

If you get stuck and you can't figure out a good book title, use the **Google Keyword Tool**. Here's the link: https://adwords.google.com/o/KeywordTool

Make sure that you **sign into your Gmail account** so you'll have full access to this keyword tool. Next, type your keyword phrase into the box (I.E…Salad Recipes), check the box below that says "*Only show ideas closely related to my search term*", and then hit the "search" button. (*Figure 8.*)

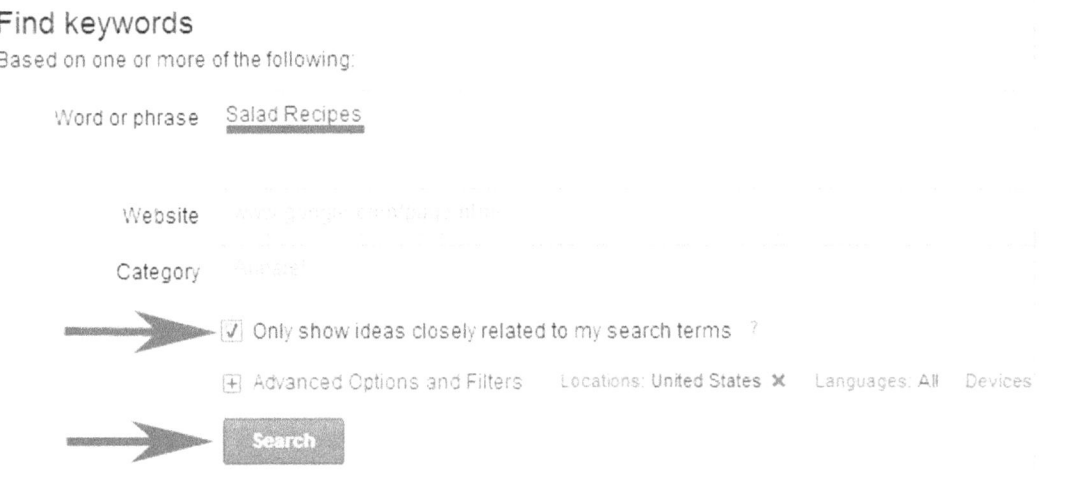

Figure 8

Scroll down and look at the keyword phrases. You can expand on those keyword ideas to help you brainstorm a few book titles. (*Figure 9.*)

Keyword	Competition	Global Monthly Searches ?	Local Monthly Searches ?
summer salad recipes ▾	Low	18,100	12,100
healthy salad recipes ▾	Low	33,100	22,200
green salad recipes ▾	Low	22,200	14,800
potato salad recipes ▾	Low	135,000	90,500
cold pasta salad recipes ▾	Medium	12,100	8,100

Figure 9

Use the information in this chapter to **brainstorm at least 5 book titles**. You can have your friends and family help you pick the best title out of the 5.

Now that you've figured out your book title, it's time to design a catchy eBook cover.

Chapter 2

How to Design a Catchy E-Book Cover

Before you design your book cover, you need to know which **colors** people like the most. Dozens of experiments have been made, and here's a list of colors that people prefer the most:

- Rank 1: Blue
- Rank 2: Red
- Rank 3: Green
- Rank 4: Violet
- Rank 5: Orange
- Rank 6: Yellow

I didn't make this information up. You can do your own research and find out for yourself. Actually, just **look at popular websites** and you'll notice their most prominent colors:

- Facebook = Blue
- Twitter = Blue
- Tumblr = Blue
- Pinterest = Red
- Google = Blue, Red, Green Yellow
- Microsoft Logo = Blue, Red, Green Yellow

Based on this information, it makes sense to **use high ranked color combinations** for your book cover. Don't select random colors that *you* personally like because the wrong colors could harm your book sales. If you want more information about the psychology of color, you can purchase a book called "*Cashvertising*" by Drew Eric Whitman.

Next, you need an image for your eBook cover. You can buy some very nice images from:

1. Getty Images - http://www.gettyimages.com
2. iStock Photo - http://www.istockphoto.com
3. Shutter Stock - http://www.shutterstock.com

A decent image should only cost $20-$30. Just make sure that you purchase an image that's "***Royalty Free***" so it's a onetime cost. I also recommend that you purchase an image that features a **person or multiple people**. For example, if you're writing a book about dog training, then you can purchase an image of an attractive young model sitting with her dog. (*Figure 10*)

Figure 10

Some **women will relate to the young model** as a projection of themselves and buy your book. Guys will also buy the book just because the model on your cover is attractive.

It works the other way around too. You could use a picture of a **handsome** well dressed guy walking his dog. Guys looking at your book cover will **envision the guy as themselves** and buy the book. Some women will buy the book just because the guy on the book cover is handsome or well dressed. (*Figure 11.*)

Title: Man with his dog at the beach

Creative image #: 56965008

License type: Royalty-free

Photographer: Image Source

Similar images:

View all

View pricing

Add to cart

Add to lightbox

Print preview i

Download prev

View terms of us

Search for mor

Resources
- Choosing the ri
- About our searc

Chat is current
- Questions? Pleas

Figure 11

If you want to be a **successful marketer**, then you need to know these details and use them to your advantage. Next time you're at your local market, walk over to the magazine stand and take a look at the magazine covers. Which magazines catch your attention first?

Figure 12

Do you look at the magazines with random designs on the cover first; or the magazines with **people** on the cover. (*Figure 12*.)

Next, to create a rough draft of your book cover, open up the "**paint**" program on your computer. It's a free program and everybody should have it on their computer. Once you have paint open, click "File" and then click "Open..." and find the image you purchased. Double click the image to import it into the paint program. (*Figure 13.*)

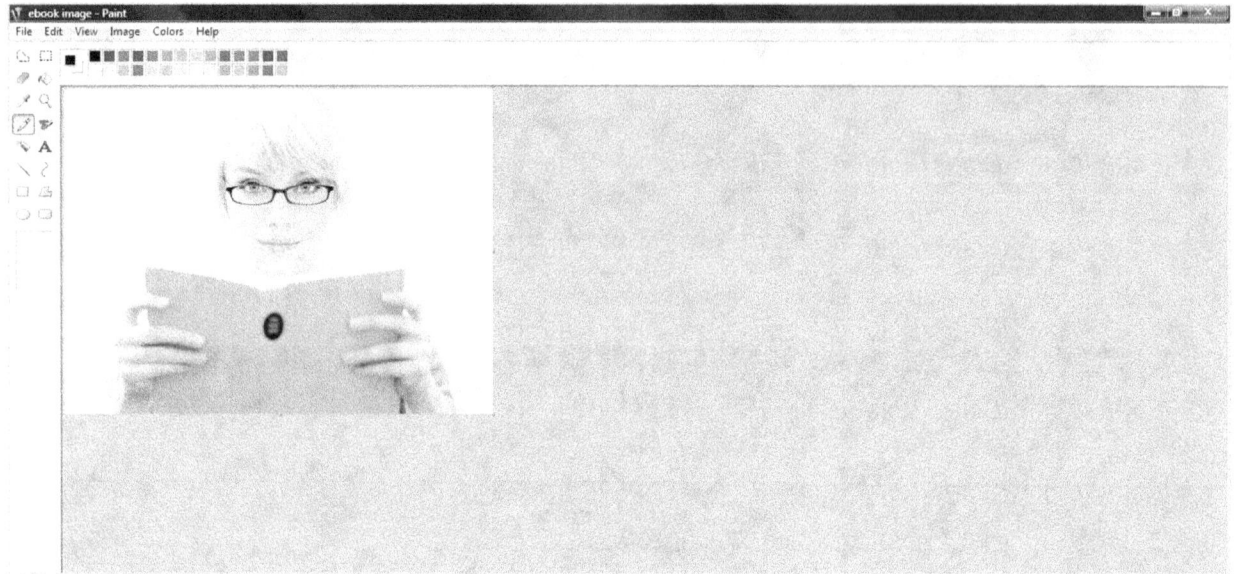

Figure 13

Now minimize the window and <u>open another paint program</u>. You should have two separate paint programs open now. In the new paint program, navigate to the top and click where it says "Images" and then click on "Attributes." (*Figure 14.*) For the width enter 500, and for the height enter 700

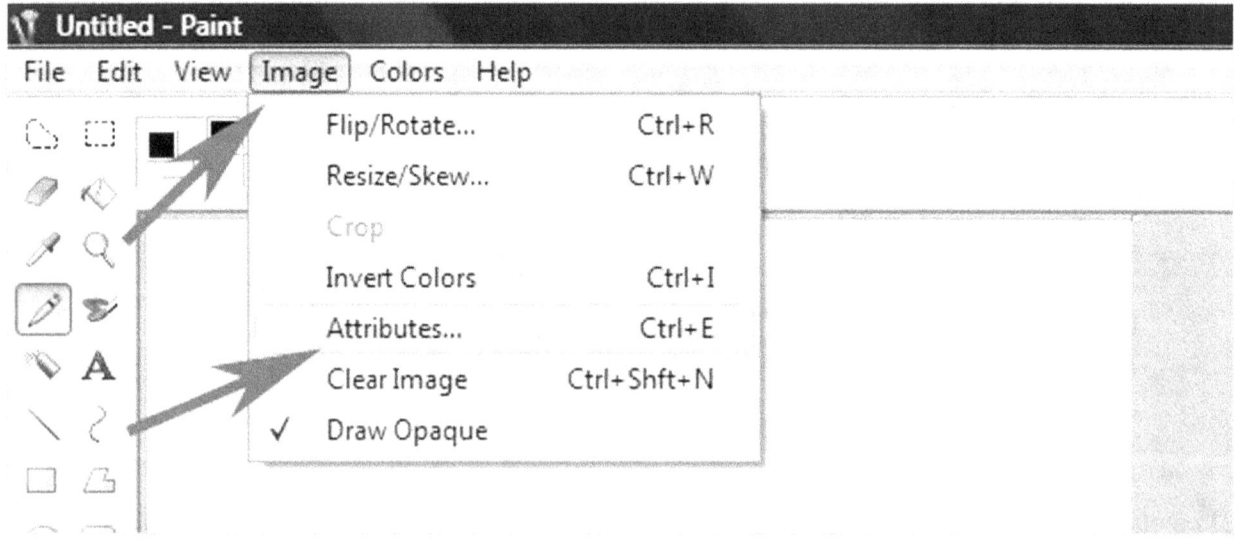

Figure 14

Now you want to click the *bucket of paint* icon which is the "**fill with color**" option. Next, choose a color from the color template or create a custom color. This will be the background color for your eBook cover. After you choose a color, click your mouse over the white space to fill it with the color you've chosen.

Now you need to add your image on top of this background. To add your image, navigate <u>back to the other paint program that contains your image</u>. At the top of the program, click "Edit" and then "Select All." This should create a broken dotted line around your image. Next click "Edit" again and then click on "Copy." (*Figure 15.*)

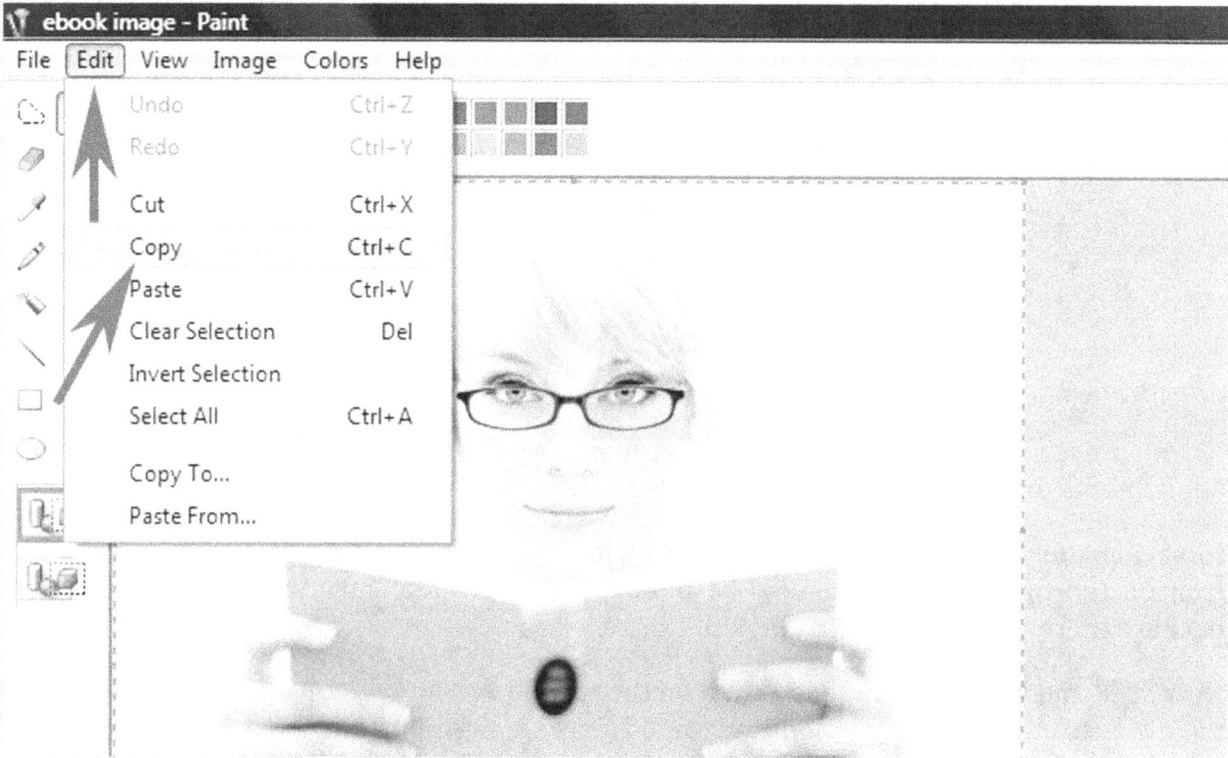

Figure 15

Now go back to your other paint program that has the colored background and click "Edit" and then click "Paste" to **paste the image over the background**. Now drag the image to the **center** of the colored background so there's some space above and below the image. You can use the space above and below the image for your text. (*Figure 16.*)

Figure 16

If your image is too wide or too narrow, just click the "attributes" tab again and make adjustments to the "width" so your image lines up with your background.

Next click the "**A**" icon on the toolbar which allows you to **write text**, and then click the last icon on the tool bar which looks like building blocks. Make sure it's the very **last icon** because there are two icons that look the same.

Now click and **hold your mouse down** on the top left corner of your book cover. Next drag your mouse *down* and to the *right* to create an area to write in your book title. Start typing in your book title, but make sure that you select a **different color so you can see your text**. You can also click the "View" tab at the top, and then select "Text Toolbar" which will give you some additional font options.

Repeat this step for the bottom area of your book cover. You can enter your *Author/Pen-name* on the bottom area. When you're done, save the book cover image to your desktop. I know this book cover doesn't look amazing, but it's just a **rough draft**. (*Figure 17.*)

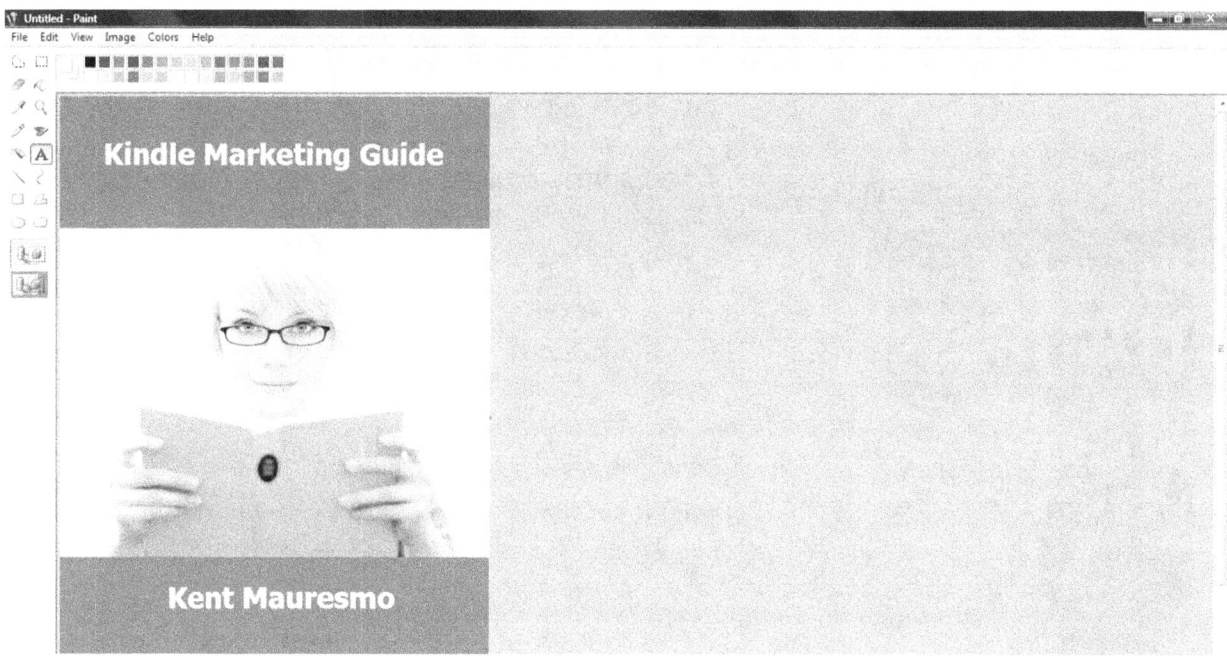

Figure 17

The whole point of this exercise is to <u>figure out which high ranked colors look good with your image</u>. Also it's a lot cheaper for a graphic designer to Photoshop your rough draft rather than creating a new eBook cover from scratch.

Here are two examples of really nice book covers that use **real people** combined with **high ranked colors**:

The Skinny Rules and over one million other books are

The Skinny Rules: The Simple, Nonnegotiable

Bob Harper ☑ (Author), Greg Critser (Author)

☆☆☆☆☆ ☑ (184 customer reviews) | 👍 Like (209)

List Price: $26.00

Price: **$15.11** & eligible for **FREE Super Saver Shippi**

You Save: $10.89 (42%)

In Stock.
Ships from and sold by **Amazon.com**. Gift-wrap available.

Want it Tuesday, Jan. 22? Order within 28 hrs 1 min, and choo:

69 new from $10.75   35 used from $8.59   1 collectible from

Formats	Amazon Price	New from
Kindle Edition	--	$13.99
Hardcover	$15.11	$10.75

In the next chapter I'll show you where to get your entire eBook formatted for Amazon Kindle including eBook cover editing.

Some people spend countless hours trying format their eBook for Amazon Kindle. Don't waste your precious time with this task.

> *"Time is more valuable than money. You can get more money,*
> *but you cannot get more time."*
> **- Jim Rohn**

Chapter 3

E-Book Formatting Strategies

If you don't have experience formatting your book for Amazon Kindle, then outsource it to a professional. If you'd like to use the same company that I use, then follow these steps:

1. Create an account at http://www.elance.com
2. Hire a company called **Access Ideas** (www.elance.com/s/accessideas). (*Figure 18*.)

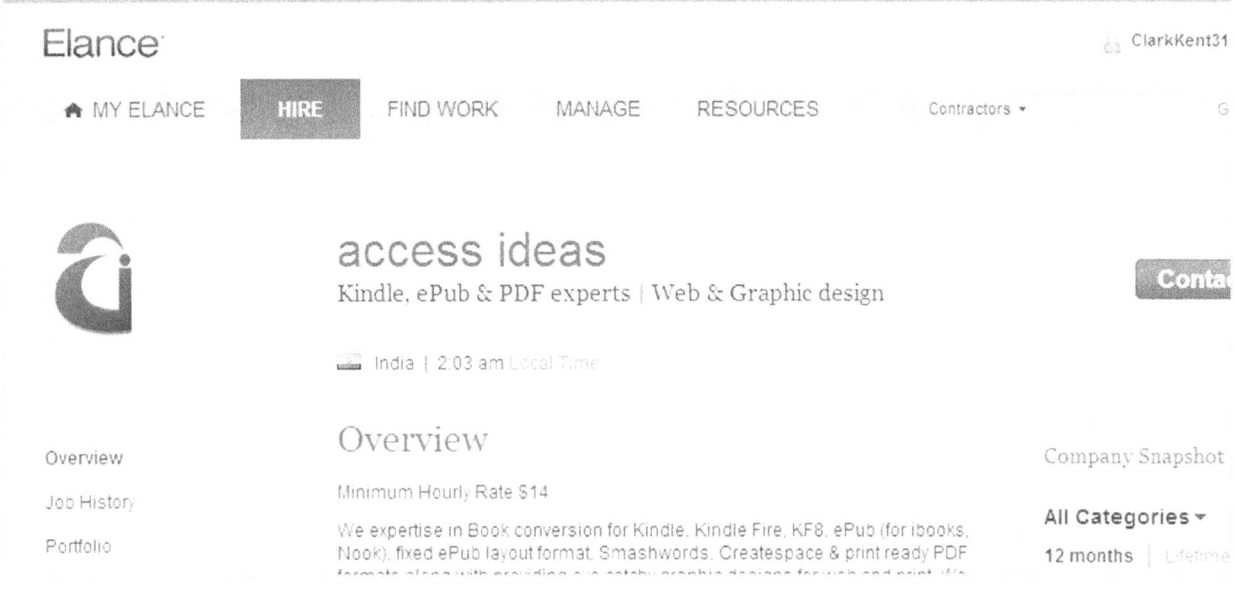

Figure 18

I've used *Access Ideas* for all of my eBooks, and they're really professional. They charge **$100-$150** depending on the length of your eBook and/or if it has a lot of pictures. They will also enhance your eBook cover (strictly as per Kindle cover requirement) with Photoshop for an additional **$40**.

There are a lot people on Elance that will offer to format your eBook for only $20. If you decide to use someone else besides *Access Ideas*, then I suggest that you ask to see eBook conversions they've completed in the past.

A large percentage of these "$20 Kindle Experts" have **never** formatted a book for Kindle. They just want to **experiment** with your book to see if they can do it or not. Don't waste your time with someone inexperienced just to save a couple dollars. You get what you pay for.

PDF Documents

While you're waiting for your *Access Ideas* (or whoever else you hired) to format your book for Kindle, this is a good time to learn about PDF documents.

Before Amazon Kindle existed, most eBooks were in PDF format. Some people still prefer reading PDF's, so you need to know how to format your eBook into a PDF document.

If you use Microsoft Word, then you can **create PDF documents very easy**. Just click the windows logo on the top left corner, click "save as", and then select the "*PDF or XPS*" option. (*Figure 19.*)

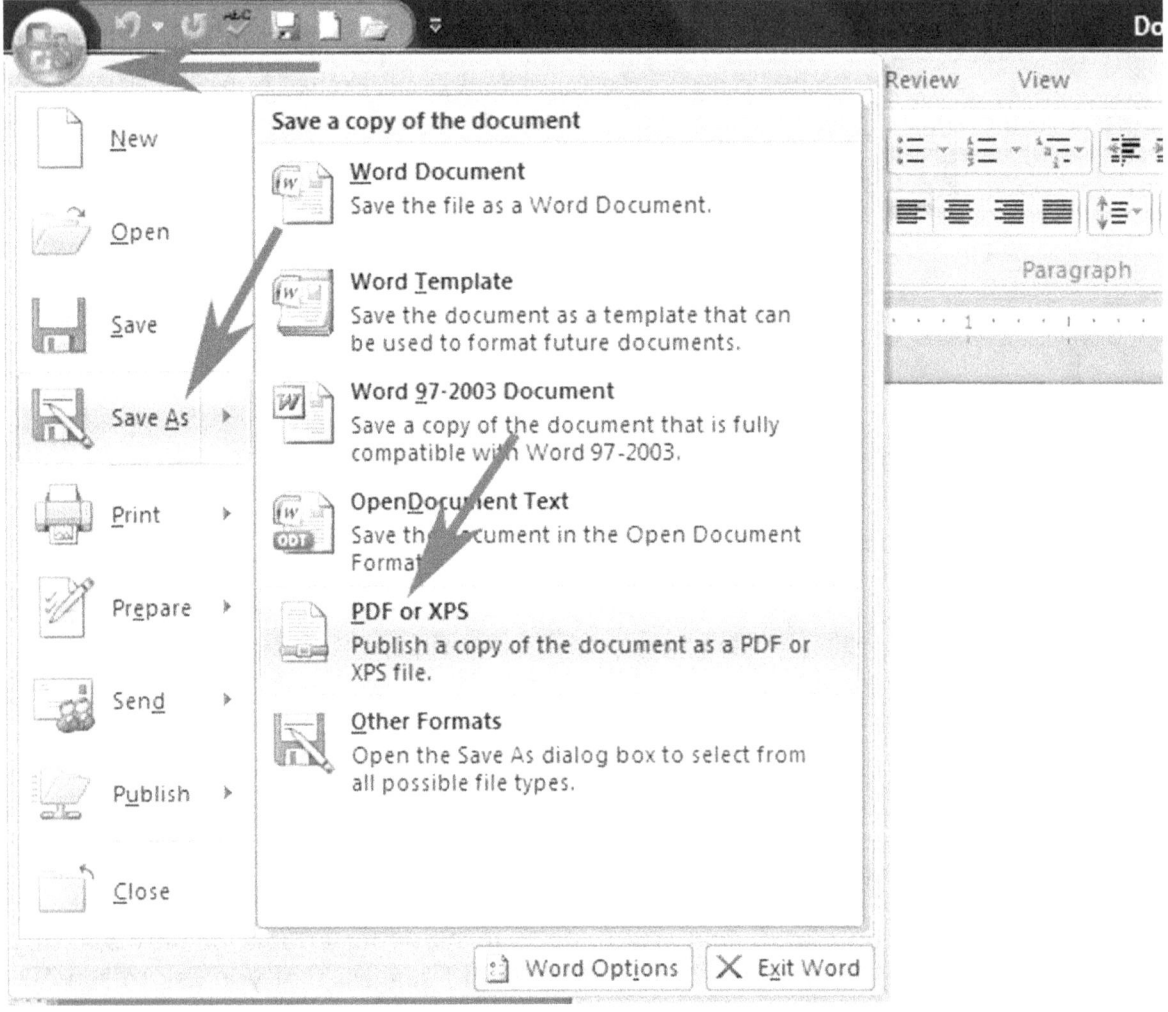

Figure 19

If you don't have Microsoft Word, you can use another free program called **Primo PDF**. I don't recommend using *Primo PDF* if you have a lot of images in your eBook. Last time I checked, the images will come out very blurry when using this program. (*Figure 20.*)

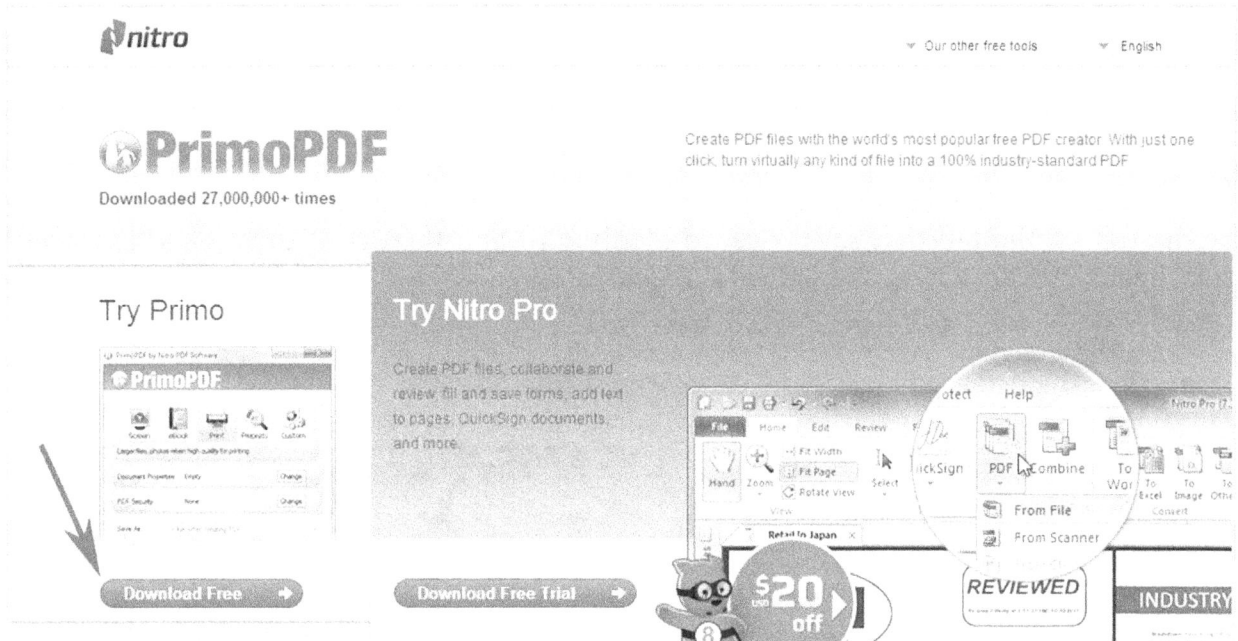

Figure 20

Now that you know how to create PDF documents, you need to sign up for two websites:

1. http://myebook.com
2. http://scribd.com

These two websites allow you to upload PDF documents that other people can read for free. Obviously you don't want to upload your entire book. Upload only a **sample** of your book and include a link that points back to your website* and your Amazon product page. ** (*Figure 21.*)

Figure 14

"Did You Like What You've Read So Far?"

You can read the rest of this eBook on Amazon.com by visiting the link below:

http://www.amazon.com/SEO-WordPress-Website-Google-ebook/dp/B0087MQTU8/

Figure 21

You're going to need a website if you're serious about marketing your eBook. Your Facebook page is not a substitute for a website. I'll talk more about this in the next chapter.

**If you haven't published your book to Amazon Kindle yet, then you won't have a product page. I'll show you how to publish your book to Amazon Kindle in a later chapter, and then you'll be able to include your Amazon link.*

It's very easy to upload your documents to MyEbook.com. After you sign up for a free account, click the tab that says "**Create Myebook**", and then click the *upload* button to select your PDF document and upload it. (*Figure 22.*)

Figure 22

Don't take this website for granted. I've had over **10,000** people read my sample book via MyEbook.com. If only 2% of those 10,000 readers decided to purchase my book, then that equals a bonus 200 books sold with almost zero effort on my part. (*Figure 23.*)

Figure 23

Scribd works the same way as MyEbook.com, but it's more like a <u>social networking site</u>. Scribd also allows you to follow other people that have the same interest as you. So if you're a fiction writer, it might be a good idea to follow people that follow other fiction books/articles in the same category as your books.

Scribd is a lot more user friendly than MyEbook.com in my opinion. You can also link your Scribd account to your Facebook and/or Twitter. To upload your documents to Scribd, just **click the blue upload icon** at the top of the website. (*Figure 24.*)

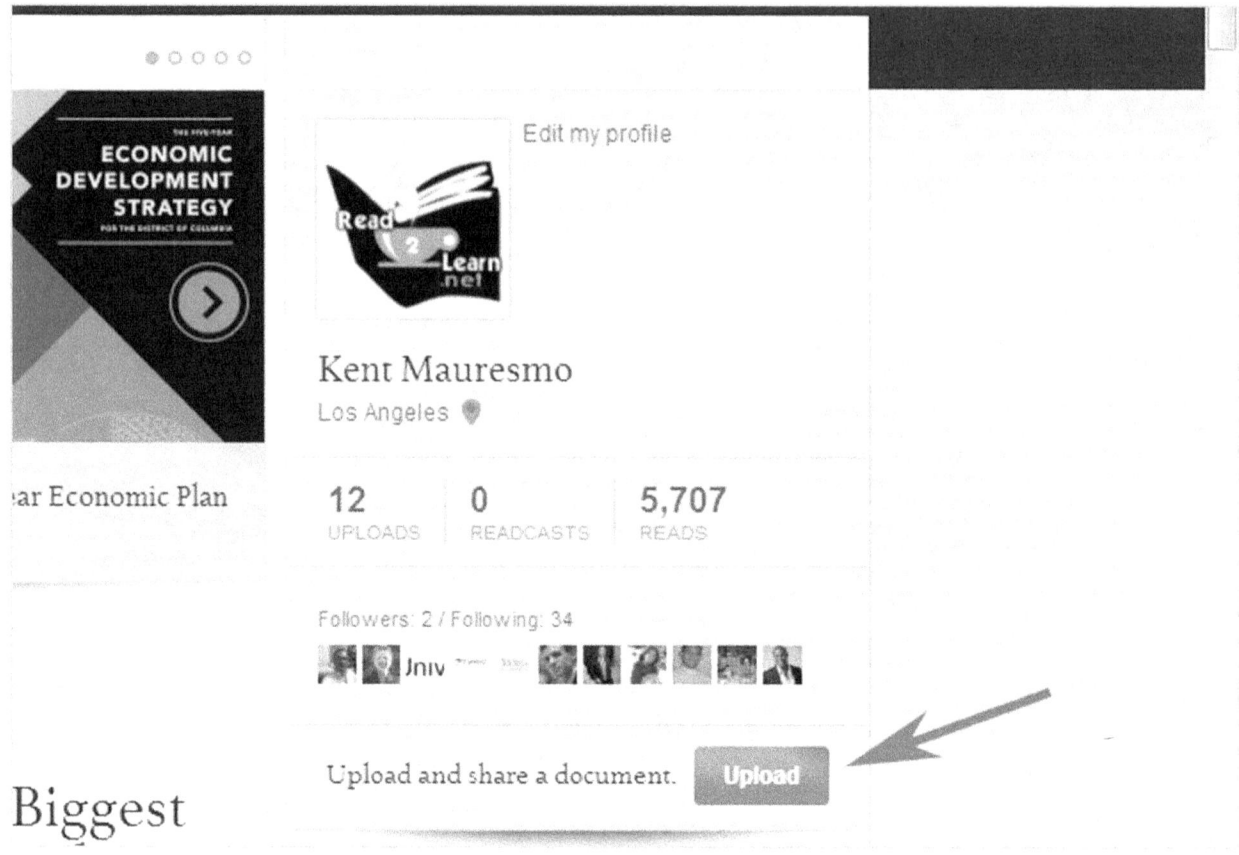

Figure 24

You can also use PDF samples on your website. For example, you can ask people to sign up for your mailing list in exchange for the first 3 chapters of your book for free.

Just remember that if you give away 2 free chapters on Scribd or MyEbook.com, it makes sense to offer 3 free chapters on your website. Some people will arrive to your website by clicking on your links from Scribd or MyEbook. It doesn't make sense for them to give you their email address in exchange for the same 2 chapters they've just read for free.

In the next chapter, I'm going to talk about building an online presence. This is a **very important step** that needs your attention before you publish your book to Amazon Kindle.

Chapter 4

How to Build an Online Presence

You need to build an online presence if you expect to sell a lot of books. The first step is to decide if you're going to use your <u>real name or a pen-name</u>.

Pen-names are important. Since you're an indie author, some people will type your name into Google before they decide if they're going to buy your book or not. If you have a common name like *John Smith,* then people will have a hard time trying to find you via Google.

Remember earlier in the book, there was an author by the name of *Karin Slaughter.* If I type her name into Google, it'll be very easy to find more information about her because her name is <u>very unique</u>. There's only one **Karin Slaughter**. (*Figure 25.*)

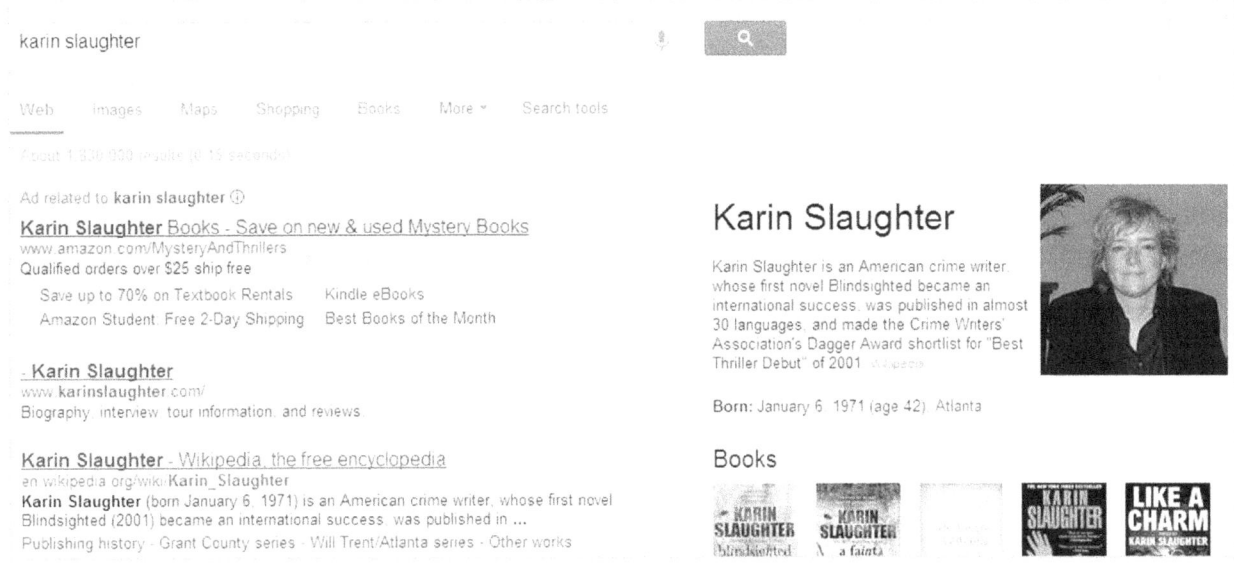

Figure 25

Have you ever noticed that most famous people have very unique names (especially last names) that no one else has? Here are a few examples:

- Leonardo DiCaprio
- Vin Diesel
- Johnny Depp

- Liam Neeson
- George Clooney

Most actors and actresses change their names because it helps them **stand out from the crowd**. So if you want to stand out from other book authors, then come up with a good pen-name. It's just a suggestion, but not necessary.

Now you need to set up a few "profile accounts" using your name and/or pen-name. Sites I recommend signing up for are:

1. Pinterest .com
2. Tumblr.com
3. Twitter.com
4. LinkedIn.com
5. YouTube.com
6. Google Plus – www.plus.google.com
7. Scribd.com

I picked these specific websites for a reason. Their easy to use and they'll show up in "Google Search" in about 2 or 3 days. That's why I suggest that you use a unique pen-name. You want to make sure that only your profiles will show up if someone types your name into Google. (i.e. *Karin Slaughter*)

Why Pinterest?

Pinterest is a social sharing website for pictures. It's a very popular website that millions of people use. The reason you should sign up for this website is because it allows people to see what your interest are.

If you write romantic vampire novels, then you can follow other people that are posting pictures of Vampires. You can also post and/or repost pictures of food that you like, cars, and vacation spots.

Make sure that you don't use Pinterest to overly advertise your book. Instead, Pinterest gives you a category that's entitled "**Books Worth Reading**." Add your book into that category along with similar bestselling books.

I actually created a board on Pinterest that has a lot of pictures of famous people and models reading books. I just added my books into that same category. (*Figure 26.*)

Figure 26

Pinterest also allows you to add your website, Facebook, and Twitter information on your profile. This will help search engines link all your profile accounts together faster.

Why Tumblr?

Tumblr is similar to Pinterest, but it looks more like a website. Most people use Tumblr to post pictures and repost other peoples pictures. You can also use Tumblr to write text just like a blog.

<u>Use Tumblr similar to the way you use Pinterest</u>. Post really nice pictures or repost other peoples pictures that you're following. (*Figure 27.*) You can also slip in a few promotions for your book, but it's not necessary.

Once again, the whole point of using this website is because it will show people that you're a normal person just like everybody else. Make sure that you use <u>your pen-name</u> as your username. The username you choose should be available if you picked a unique name.

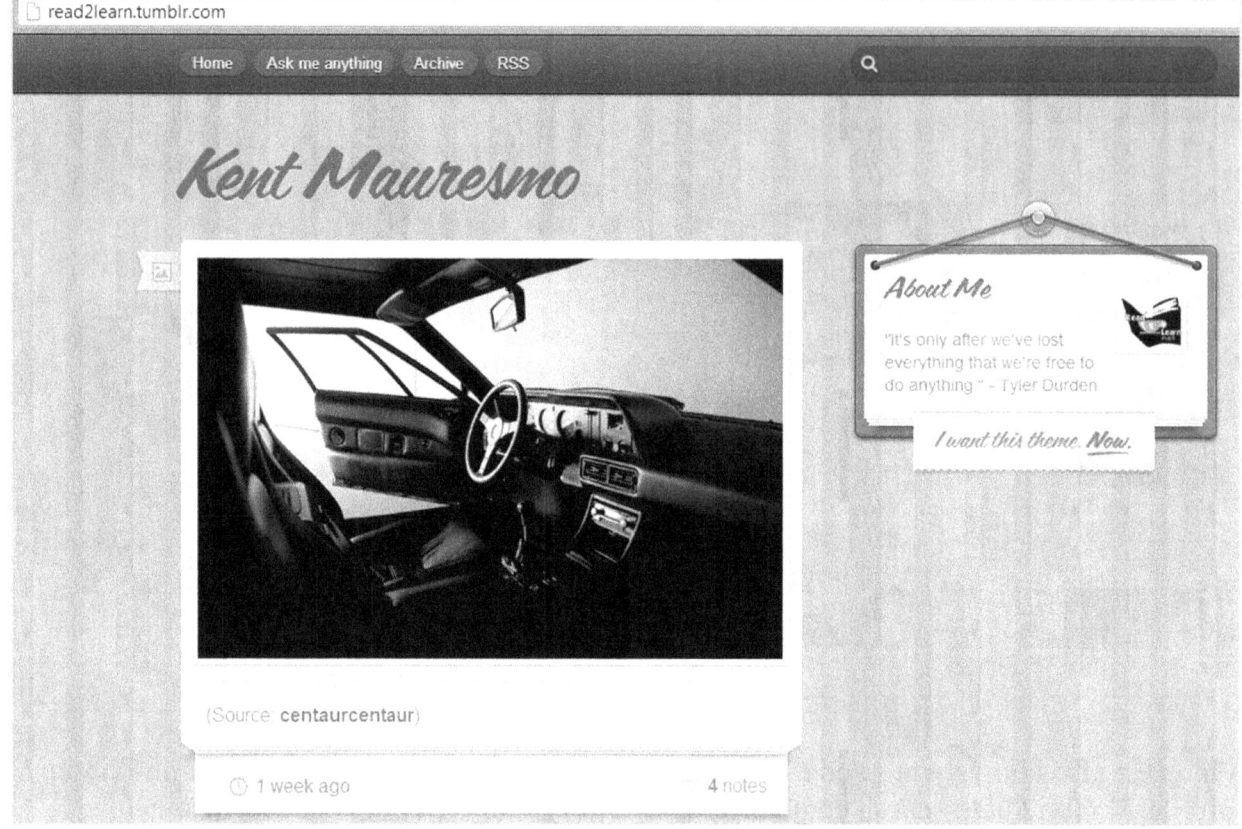

Figure 27

The Correct Way To Use Twitter

Twitter is a really good website if you use it correctly. Twitter allows you to post short status updates about anything you want. You can also include links within your status updates for people to click on.

To use Twitter correctly, <u>don't post too many status updates that have links</u>. If all your status updates have links, then people will think you're a spammer. Most Twitter users are just bored and they want to read funny updates from people. Also, most people will only click on a link within a status update if it leads to a funny picture, video, or article.

People don't use Twitter to go shopping for books so don't advertise your book too much there. Instead of aggressively advertising, just talk to people on their like a normal person. If you want to find people with similar interests as you, then use the "**search**" feature at the top of Twitter. You'll find thousands of people posting interesting status updates that you can respond too.

Twitter allows you to **add your website address on your profile page**, so there's no need to post a link to your book every 5 minutes. If people think you're interesting, they'll view your profile and click on your websites link. (*Figure 28*.)

Figure 28

Post a few things on Twitter per day, and follow interesting people that share your same interests. Twitter serves as <u>social proof</u>, so it a good idea to get a lot of followers. It will only take 3 or 4 days for *Access Ideas* to format your book, and there's no way you can get a couple thousand followers that fast on Twitter.

You can get a lot of followers on Twitter fast by outsourcing the task to Elance for probably $20. As soon as you have about 1000 followers, then other people will start following you naturally. It's the bandwagon effect.

LinkedIn Profile

LinkedIn is a **professional social network** where you can advertise your skills and brag about your accomplishments. LinkedIn reminds me of Facebook because you can't connect with people unless you know them. That's one of the reasons I don't like LinkedIn, but it's still good to sign up for the website.

LinkedIn is like a virtual resume/business card. You can also connect LinkedIn to Twitter and your website which is really good. To tell you the truth, a lot of these social networking websites are useless for the most part. They all seem to do the exact same thing in my opinion.

I only know a few people that actively use LinkedIn, but it's still <u>good to set up a</u> profile as **social proof**. It looks good when someone types your name into Google, and the search results display your profile to LinkedIn. It looks like you mean business!

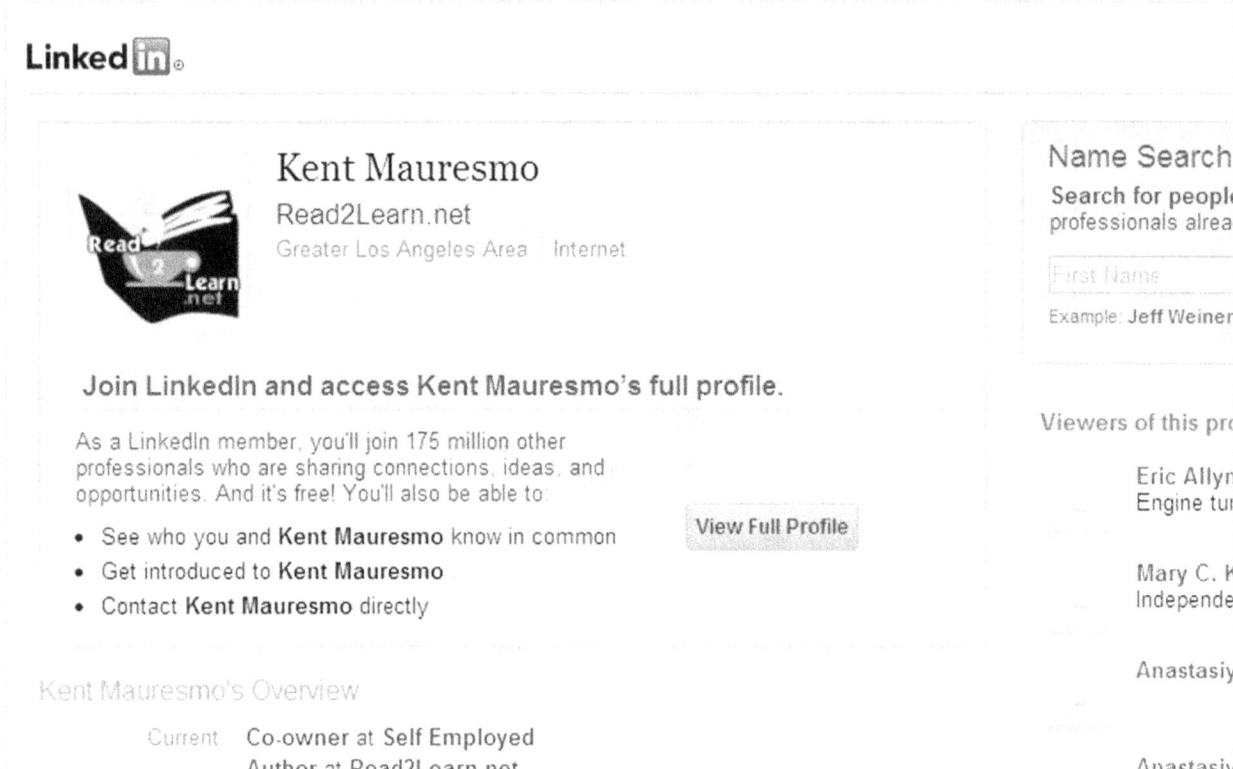

YouTube: Create a Commercial

Everybody watches videos on Youtube including you! I'm sure you already have a YouTube account, but create another one using your pen-name.

Now you need to upload a couple videos fast, and you need your videos to look professional. Sign up for a website called *Animoto.com* and create an HD slide show video advertising your book. You can create a slide show on Animoto that almost looks like a real commercial if you use it correctly. (*Figure 29.*)

Figure 29

I also recommend that you pay a little extra so you can <u>upgrade your videos to 720 High Definition</u>. If you upload a poor quality video to YouTube, then people will assume your book is poor quality too.

Also, it doesn't matter if a lot of people watch this video on YouTube or not. You'll still need this video later for your <u>Amazon profile</u> which is the real reason why I'm telling you to create it.

After you upload the video to YouTube, you should "favorite" and "like" other interesting videos that you like. If somebody decides to check out your YouTube profile, they will get a chance to see what type of music, movies, or videos you like to watch. As I mentioned earlier, this will show people that you're a <u>real person</u> that watches funny videos on YouTube too.

You can share the videos you like on Twitter by clicking the "**Share**" button under the YouTube videos. You can also automatically link your YouTube account to Twitter so every time you "*Like*" a video, it'll be shared with your friends on Twitter.

Create a Profile with Google+

Since most people will type your name into Google, it makes sense to create a profile with *Google+*. *Google+* is like Facebook except it's more professional.

I personally think *Google+* is the perfect mix between Facebook and LinkedIn and it's easy to use. Also, if someone is signed into *Google+* and they type your name into Google, there's a 50/50 chance that your information might populate on the top right corner with a link to your Google+ profile. (*Figure 30.*)

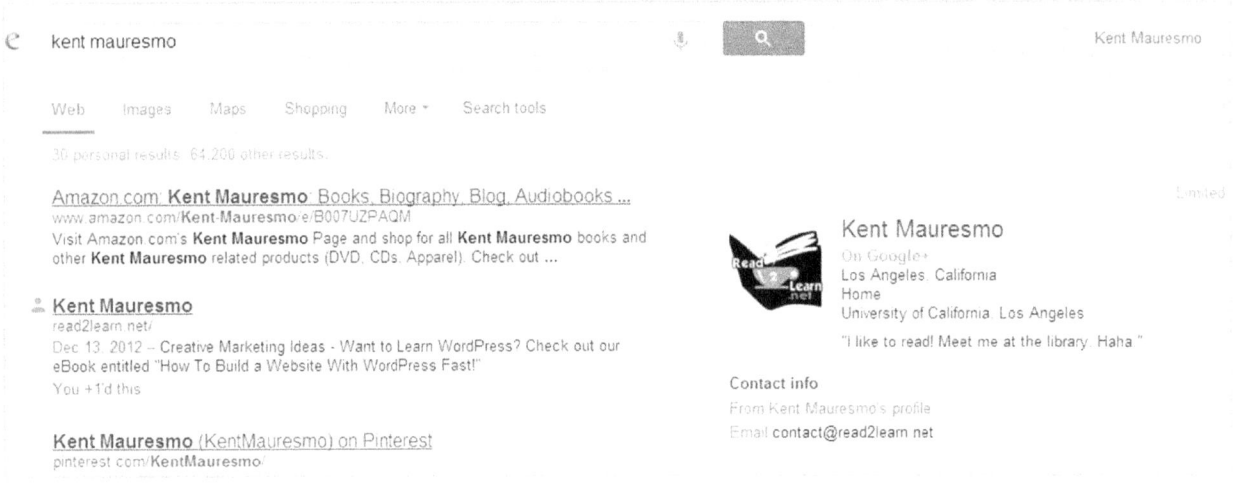

Figure 30

Do You Need a Website?

YES! **You definitely need a website**. How can you expect people to take you serious if you use your Facebook page as your website? It's not that hard to create a simple blog or website. You can actually have a website up in less than 24 hours that looks really professional.

Your website is your home base. You can use your website to:

1. Give out samples of your book.
2. Upload videos.
3. Announce upcoming books.
4. Interact with your readers.
5. Write blog posts to show your writing style.
6. Create a mailing list.
7. Connect to YouTube, Twitter, Facebook, LinkedIn, Tumblr, Pinterest..etc.

Your readers need a central way to connect with you, and a website is the solution. **Every professional author has a real website** that links to all their other profile accounts. The best way to set up a website fast is to use the *WordPress* platform. I'm not talking about WordPress.com because that's the free version like Blogger.com. Most free platforms have limited functions and they look cheap.

I recommend using the WordPress.org platform because its professional and it's easy to set up. (*WordPress.com* and *WordPress.org* are different.) If you're interested in setting up a website fast, then you should check out our WordPress eBook when you're done reading this one.

I know what some of you are thinking. Probably something like, "*Kent, this seems like **hard work**. I don't know if I want to make a website or set up all these silly profile accounts. It's just too hard..*"

Keep in mind that anything that's considered "hard work" separates the **winners** from the losers. 95% of people usually give up when something seems mildly difficult. The other 5% will always cash a bigger check because they're willing to do something that other people are too lazy to do.

> *"I'm a firm believer in luck, and I've found that the harder I work, the luckier I get."*
> **-Thomas Jefferson**

Chapter 5

Amazon Kindle: How To Check For Formatting Errors

By now, *Access Ideas* should've completed your eBook conversion for Amazon Kindle. Before you upload your eBook to Amazon, you need to make sure that it's formatted **correctly** and that it'll look good on eReader devices.

To see what your eBook will look like to potential readers; download Kindle for PC and/or MAC. Here are the links:

- www.amazon.com/**kindleforpc** (Download link for **PC**)
- www.amazon.com/**kindleformac** (Download link for **MAC**)

If you have a PC, you can also download a program called *"Mobipocket Reader."* This program will also allow you to open your kindle eBook to see what it'll look like. Here's the download link:

- http://www.mobipocket.com/en/downloadSoft/ProductDetailsReader.asp

After you have these programs installed, navigate to the folder on your computer that contains your eBook file. It should be a ".**prc**" file that looks like a tiny book. Next:

1. *Right click* on your book file.
2. Select *"Open with.."*
3. Then select the *"Kindle"* option to view your book. (*Figure 31.*)

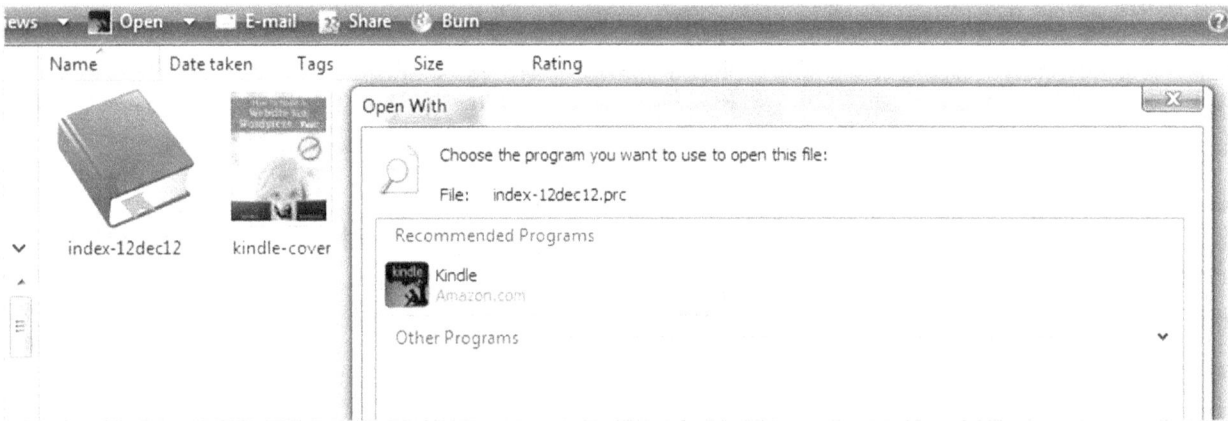

Figure 31

You should be able to look through your eBook using the Kindle program. If Kindle won't upload your book, then use *Mobipocket Reader* instead. To open your book in Mobipocket:

1. Double click the *Mobipocket Reader* icon on your desktop to open the software.
2. On the top navigation bar, click *File*, then *Open*, navigate to the folder that has your book file, and then double click on the file to open your eBook in Mobipocket. (*Figure 32.*)

Figure 32

Sometimes the Amazon Kindle software won't allow you to import your book, but the *Mobipocket* method works 100% of the time. That's why I want to give you both options just in case the Kindle software is having a bad day.

If your book looks good, then let's head over the Amazon to get it published. This is the fun part!

Amazon Kindle: Self-Publishing Strategy Guide

To publish your book on Amazon, you have to sign up for an account by going to: http://kdp.amazon.com.

To create an account, you will need to provide your bank account information (if you want your money direct deposited into your account), and you'll need to provide an SSN or EIN for tax purposes.

Once you're signed in, click the words "**Bookshelf**" on the top left corner, and then click the orange button that says, "**Add new title**." (*Figure 33.*)

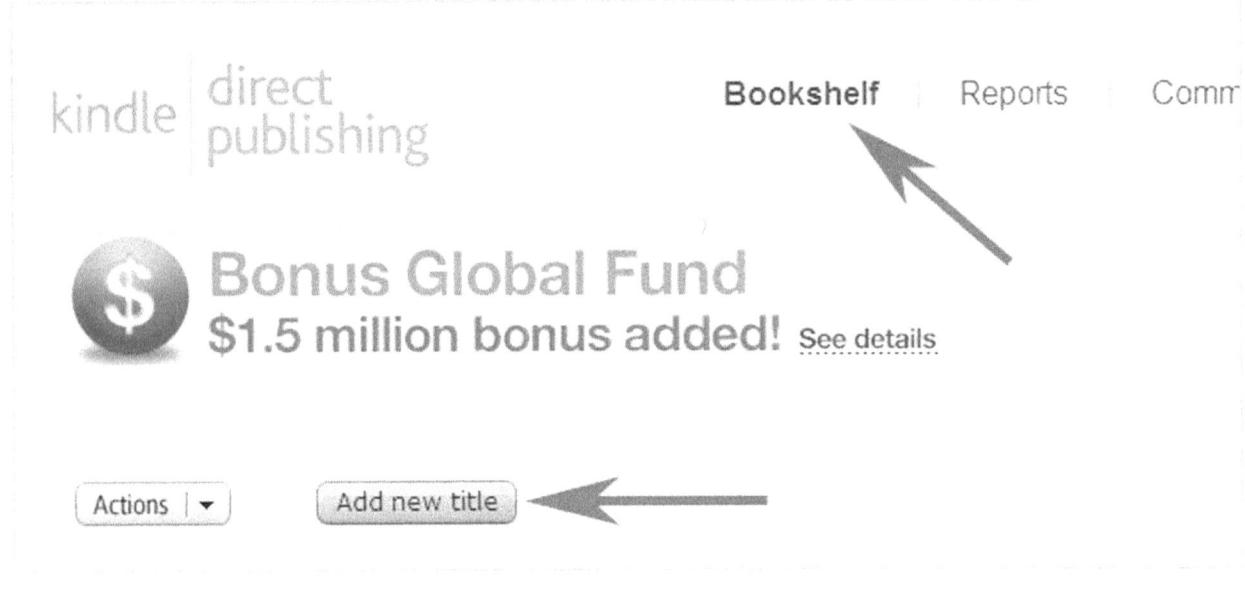

Figure 33

Next you'll be taken to a screen where you can enter information about your book. All the information required for your book will be self-explanatory. If you're confused about something, they have links that say "***What's this?***" that you can click on. Those links will open a small pop-up box that will explain the different sections for you.

KDP Select
The first option you'll have is to check a box to enroll your book into **KDP Select**. Check that box! KDP Select will allow readers to borrow your book from the Kindle Owners Lending Library. You'll still get paid a percentage when people borrow your book, so it's a win/win situation.

Also when you enroll your book into KDP Select, you'll be able to promote your book as FREE for up to 5 days within a 90 day period. I know it sounds silly to give away you book for FREE, but this works to your advantage for 2 reasons:

1. When a lot of people download your book for free, your book will move up the **Top Free** best sellers list.
2. The *Top Free* best sellers list runs parallel to the *Top Paid* best sellers list. (*Figure 34.*) So now you have more eyeballs on your book which will get you even MORE free downloads. When your free promotion is over, Amazon will bump you up on the ***Top Paid*** best sellers list which will equal more sales.

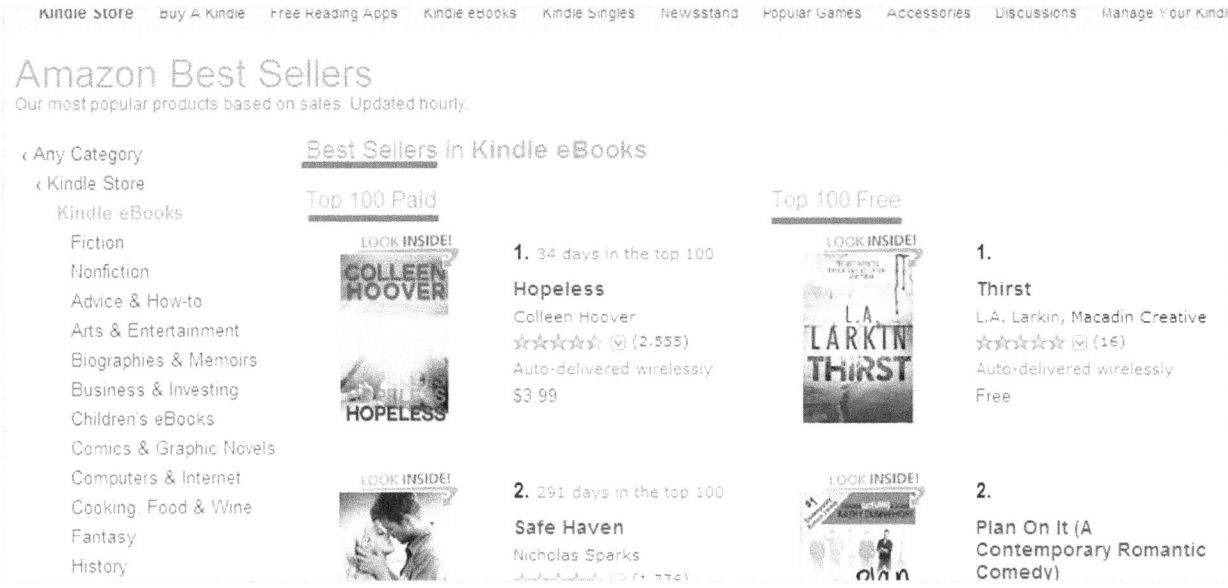

Figure 34

Enter Your Book Details

Next you have to enter your books details. The most important fields here are your **Title**, **Description**, and **Book Contributors**. You should have your title figured out by now, so go ahead and enter your title into the "Book Name" field. Try to avoid adding extra words into that field. Amazon even gives you a disclaimer saying to only enter the exact title.

As mentioned earlier, a lot of people will try to describe their book within the "Book Name" field. That's very confusing and it looks tacky. If your book title is unnecessarily long, **Amazon might not publish your book**. So make sure that your book title is short and direct to the point. The description field is where you want to describe your book.

Book Details: Description

You're allowed to use up to 4000 characters in the description field, and you should take advantage of this. **Write a very long description** about your book and go into details. If you can, use all 4000 characters because the description field is your sales pitch.

If you're a **fiction author**, obviously you don't want to give away the entire book within the description field. You can possibly use the description field to describe the characters in your book and peak your readers interest. This will give people a chance to see your writing style.

You have to go above and beyond to convince people to buy your books. <u>You cannot write a 3 sentence book description</u> (like the famous authors do) and expect your books to sell. There are a lot of horrible indie books on Amazon, so some people think twice before purchasing a book even if it's only 99 cents.

If you're a **non-fiction** author like me, then you need to <u>fully describe</u> the benefits of your book. You have to use the description field to let your readers know exactly what they'll get from each chapter. If your book has any bonus material, make sure to include details about the bonus in the description field.

<u>The longer your description, the more convincing you'll be</u>. A lot of people won't even read the entire description. They'll just see how long it is and think, "*Wow! This book must be the real deal! Look at how much information it has!*"

On the other hand, if the description for your non-fiction book is really **short**, then people will think that your book is **short** too with little to no information. Also, don't brag about yourself within the description area. If readers want to find out how "amazing" you are, they can click on your *Author Central Profile* which I'll talk about later.

If you decide to write a long description, make sure that you only write a few sentences and then start a new paragraph. If you write a wall of text in the description field, no one will read it because it will look too overwhelming.

Book Contributors

This is where you **add your pen-name** that you created earlier. Click the button that says "Add Contributors" and you'll be able to enter the name of authors, editors, illustrators, photographers, or anybody else that has contributed to your book. (*Figure 35.*)

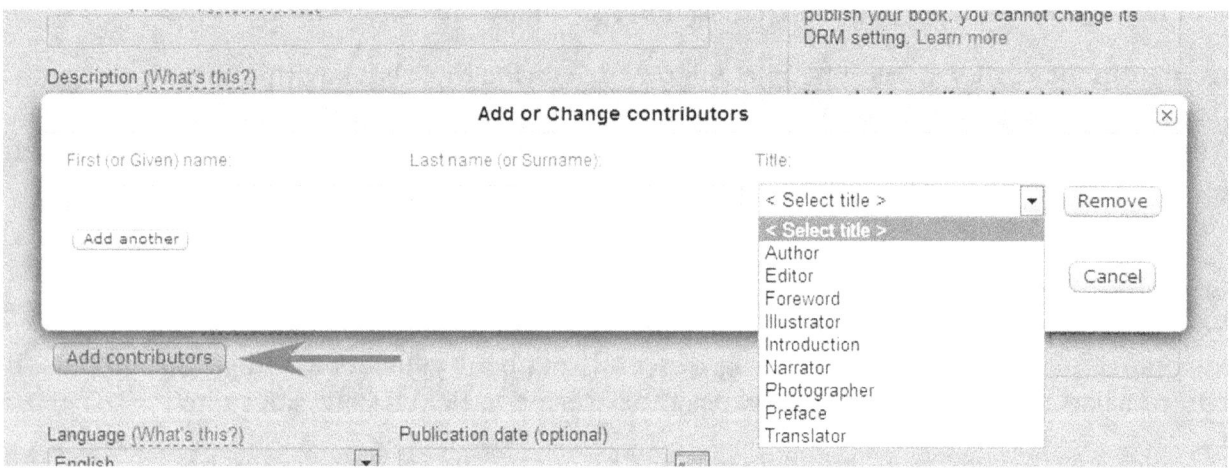

Figure 35

It's very important that you **use your pen-name as the author**. If you're stubborn and want to use your real name too, then just add another author as a book contributor and enter your real name.

The "*Profile Accounts*" that you set up earlier should show up in the Google search results by now. So if somebody decides to perform a Google search about you, the first page of

Google should be filled with information about you from reputable sites. This will almost always **encourage a skeptical buyer** to purchase your book!

When a potential reader sees that you have a professional website, Twitter account with lots of followers, LinkedIn, Pinterest, Tumblr, *Google+*, and a YouTube channel with a professional video, you're good to go. That's a lot of **social proof** for the average person to ignore.

DISCLAIMER: All the social proof in the world won't help you if you're publishing rehashed and/or junk books.

Next, below the contributors section you'll see a few options for **Language**, **Publication date**, **Publisher**, and **ISBN** (*Figure 36.*) This is very simple to fill out:

- Language: English (90% of the time)
- Publication date: Leave this blank. Amazon fills this in when your book goes live.
- Publisher: Enter your company name or your Pen-name.
- ISBN: Leave this blank. You don't need an ISBN to publish a <u>digital</u> book on Amazon.

Figure 36

Below this section is an area where you **verify your publishing rights**. Check the second option to verify that you hold the necessary publishing rights for your book.

Target Your Book to Customers

This is where you can **add categories** for your book. Some people are taught to game the system to get on the bestsellers list. What they do is categorize their book into a weird or obscure category so that they'll only have to sell 2 or 3 books to get on the best sellers list.

This is a **flawed strategy**.

If you only sell 2 or 3 books per month, then you don't actually have a bestseller yet. So ask yourself, do you want to become a bestselling author, or just pretend like you're one?

Amazon will send out emails to promote your book to readers that have already purchased books within your category. So if you categorize your book incorrectly, then Amazon will promote your book to the **wrong** group of people via email.

You can select up to 2 categories, so choose them wisely. (*Figure 37.*) You can also search Amazons bestsellers list if you need help selecting categories. Click on a few books that you feel are similar to yours, and categorize your book same way.

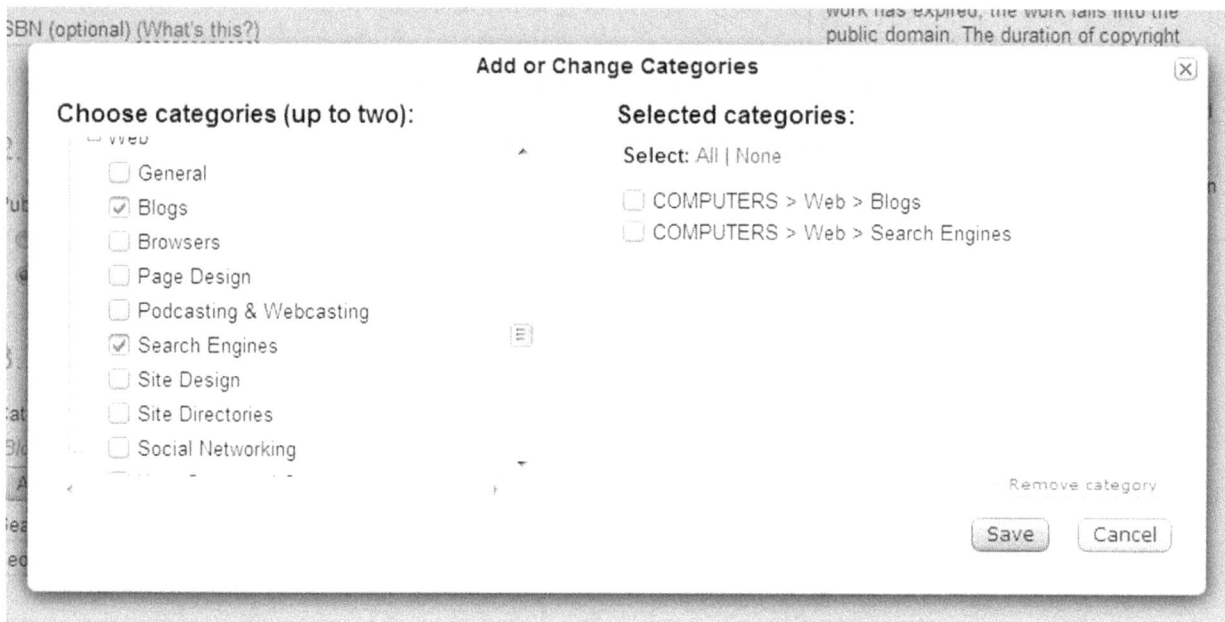

Figure 37

Under the category section, you'll see a section for **Search Keywords**. You have the option to enter up to 7 search keywords for your book. *Search Keywords* are search terms that cause your book to appear in Amazons search results. Make sure that you separate your keywords with commas.

There are 3 ways that you can come up with Keywords for your book:

1. You can **guess** which keywords people will use to find your book.
2. Use the **Google Keyword Tool** which I mentioned earlier in this book.
3. Search Amazon bestsellers list for books similar to yours. Next scroll down past the book reviews, and look for a section that says "***Tags Customers Associate with This Product.***" There you'll see keywords that customers have associated

with the book. You can use some of those tags as search keywords for your book. (**Tag feature may or may not be available as Amazon is making changes.*)

Next upload your book cover which is very simple. After that you'll have to select a digital rights management option (DRM). Click the box that says "*Do NOT enable digital rights management.*" DRM (*Digital Rights Management*) is intended to inhibit unauthorized distribution of the Kindle file of your book, but don't worry about that.

If someone's really determined to steal your book and/or read it for free, they'll find a way. How many times have you given a paperback book to your friend to read? Guess what? That's unauthorized distribution! Hah! It won't hurt your sales, so don't worry about it.

Next browse for your book and upload it. After your book is uploaded, you'll see the words "**Upload and conversion successful!**" with a green check mark next to it. Now scroll down and click the "**preview book**" button to see what your book will look like on the Black n' White Kindle. If it looks good, then click the orange button on the bottom of the page that says "Save and Continue."

Publishing Territories, Royalty's, and Pricing

Now it's time to verify your publishing territory. You can either select "*Worldwide rights*" or "*Individual Territories.*"

If you select *worldwide rights*, Amazon will make your eBook available to everybody in the world. If you decide to select *individual territories*, then you can select which countries and/or territories that you want to sell your eBook. Obviously you want your eBook to be available to everybody in the world, so select the *worldwide rights* option.

Next you have to select a **royalty option** for your book. You can choose between 35% and 70%. You must price your book between **$2.99** and **$9.99** to qualify for the 70% royalty option. (*Figure 38.*)

8. Choose Your Royalty

Please select a royalty option for your book. (What's this?)

- ○ 35% Royalty
- ◉ 70% Royalty

	List Price	Royalty Rate	Delivery Costs	Estimated Royalty
Amazon.com	$ 4.97 USD Must be between $2.99 and $9.99	35% (Why?)	n/a	$1.74
		70%	$0.34	$3.24
India (sold on Amazon.com) (What's this?)	☑ Set IN price automatically based on US price $4.97	70%	$0.28	$3.28

Figure 38

Some people like to price their books at 99 cents, but I think that's another flawed marketing strategy. A few **years ago**, a book priced at 99 cents looked like an amazing deal to customers and they sold very well.

Unfortunately, a ton of "*make money online*" guys turned their focus to Amazon Kindle and guess what happened? They saturated the market with rehashed public domain books with unprofessional formatting! Guess how much they sold their books for? **99 cents!**

So now when people see an eBook for 99 cents, it doesn't seem like an amazing deal anymore. Instead they see it as a potential waste of 99 cents and they'll actually look for a more expensive book.

Think about it; if you were publishing a lot of books that you knew were absolutely horrible, then you would price them at 99 cents too because that's all they're worth. If you feel that you actually wrote a good book then there's no way you'd price it so low and people realize this.

So if you want to give your readers an amazing deal, just **price your book at $2.99 firm!** If you're a non-fiction writer like me, then you can price your books at $4.97 too! $3-$5 is not a lot of money to ask for a good book.

As of right now, the bestselling book on Amazon Kindle is "*Fifty Shades of Grey*" by E L James. Her kindle eBook is currently priced at **$9.99** which tells me that people don't mind spending $10 for an eBook...FACT! So if you're priced at $2.99, that's a steal!

Even Amazon wants you to price your book at least at $2.99 which is why they'll give you a higher royalty at that price. Let's try to leave the 99 cents pricing strategy to the scammers, and it will benefit **everybody** in the end.

Next you'll see a box that says "*Allow lending for this book*." Check that box if it's not already checked. *Kindle Book Lending* will allow users to lend your book after purchasing to their friends and family for a duration of 14 days. Don't worry about this hurting your sales. You have to allow people to share your book because it's **good for marketing**. (*Figure 39.*)

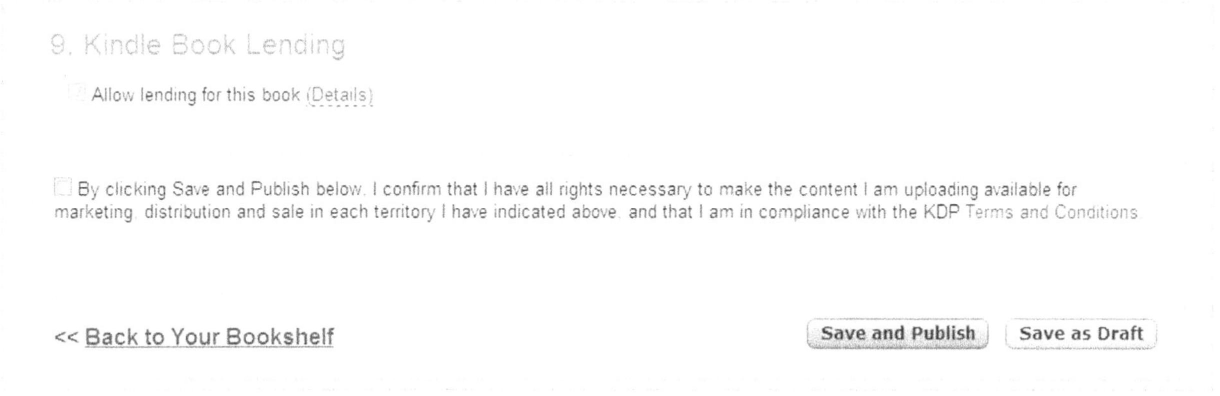

9. Kindle Book Lending

Allow lending for this book (Details)

By clicking Save and Publish below, I confirm that I have all rights necessary to make the content I am uploading available for marketing, distribution and sale in each territory I have indicated above, and that I am in compliance with the KDP Terms and Conditions

<< Back to Your Bookshelf   Save and Publish   Save as Draft

Figure 39

Lastly, there's a *Terms and Conditions* box that you have to check. Read the terms and conditions page, and if you're in agreement, just click the orange button that says "***Save and Publish***." A window will pop up that says your book will be published within 24-48 hours.

Once your eBook is published, you'll receive an email with a link to your product page. Now you're making some good progress, but you're not done yet! Let's go to the next step.

Chapter 6

How to Create a Professional Author Central Profile

To create an Author Central Profile, go to **https://authorcentral.amazon.com** and click the "*Join Now*" button to create an account. You should use the same email address that you used to sign up for Kindle Direct Publishing. It will make the process easier.

Once you're signed into your Author Central account, you'll see a few tabs along the top row. The tabs will read: *Home*, *Books*, *Profile*, *Sales Info*, *Customer Reviews*, and *Help*.

The first thing you should do is add your book to your Author Central profile. To do this click the "*Books*" tab at the top, click the "*Add Book(s)*" button, and then search for your book. You can search for your book by typing in your books title or using your Author/Pen-name. (*Figure 40.*)

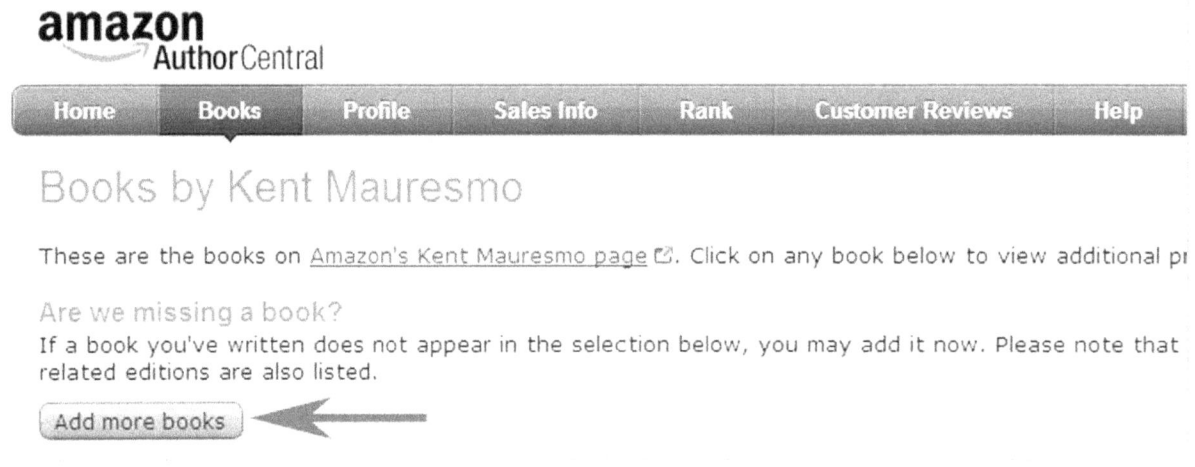

Figure 40

After you add your books, **Amazon will verify** that your email address matches the email account to your Kindle Publishing account. That's why you need to use the same email address when signing up to Author Central.

Next, click the "*Profile*" tab at the top which is the most important area. The first thing you need to do on this page is to enter your **biography**. Just like your books description, you should make your biography as long as possible. The longer your biography, the more convincing you'll be as an author. You should also enter your websites address within the biography section. (*Figure 41.*)

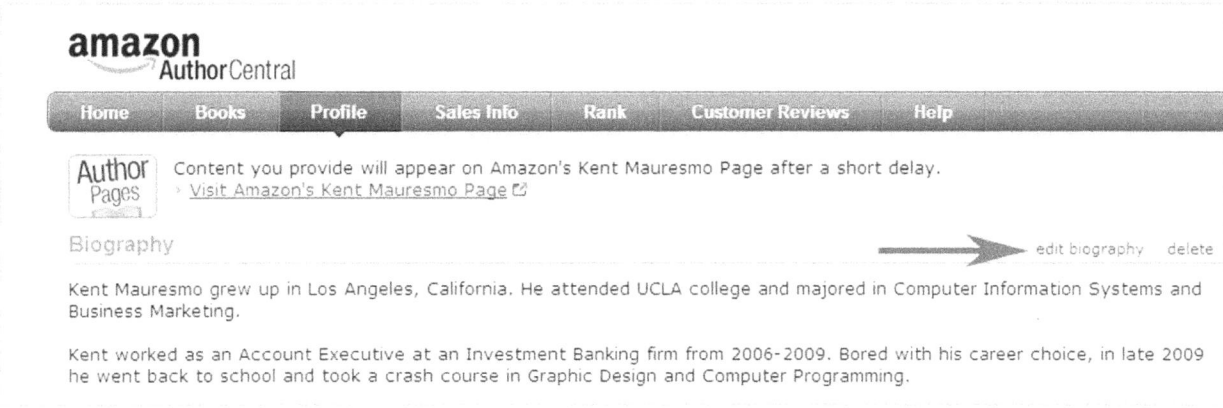

Figure 41

If you look below the biography area, you'll see a section that says "**Blogs.**"(*Figure 42.*) Within this section of Author Central, they will request your **RSS feed address** from your blog/website. If you've read our other book, then you know what an RSS Feed is and you already have one. If not, you can get one at www.feedburner.com

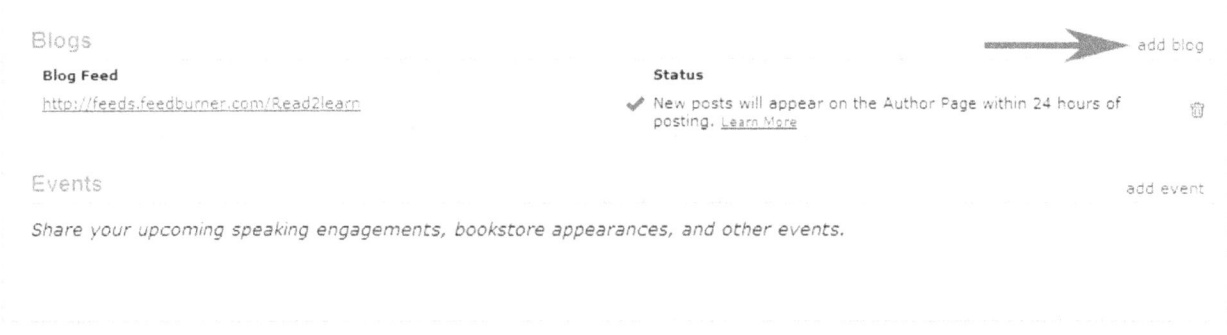

Figure 42

To find your RSS feed address, go to your website and click on your RSS button. (*Figure 43.*) Your RSS feed address will show up in the address bar of your web browser. Just **copy and paste your RSS feed address into your Author Central profile**.

When potential readers visit your Author Central profile, Amazon will display your three most recent blog posts. Most people miss this step because they don't have a website. It takes less than 10 seconds to add your RSS feed, and you're done.

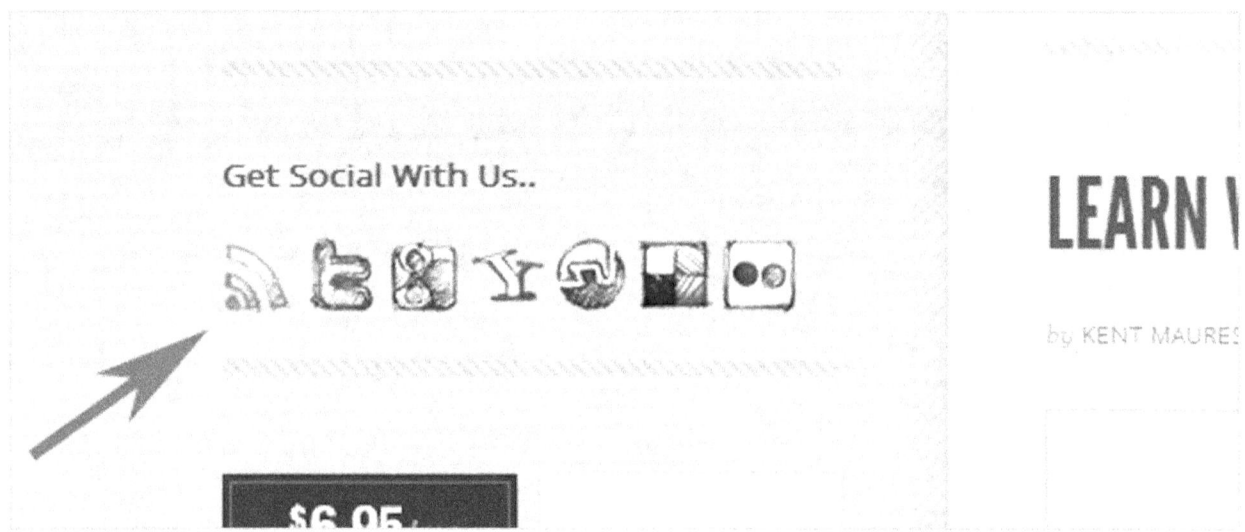

Figure 43

Below the blog section is an area that says "**Events**." This is where you can share your upcoming speaking engagements, bookstore appearances, and other events. If you're an indie author just starting out, then I doubt you'll be doing any bookstore appearances! You can skip this section, and move along to the top right corner of Author Central.

On the top right, you'll see an area that says "**Author Page URL**." Here you can customize your link to your Author page on Amazon. It's best to customize your link using your pen-name or your websites name. You are limited to one author page URL, so make sure that you set this up correctly the first time. If for some reason you need to change your URL, you'll need to contact customer service to request a new one. (*Figure 44.*)

Figure 44

Next, you can upload photos for your profile. **Upload photos** of yourself or photos that represent you best as an author. Obviously you shouldn't upload any obscene photos or images that infringe on someone else's trademark/copyright. (*Figure 45.*)

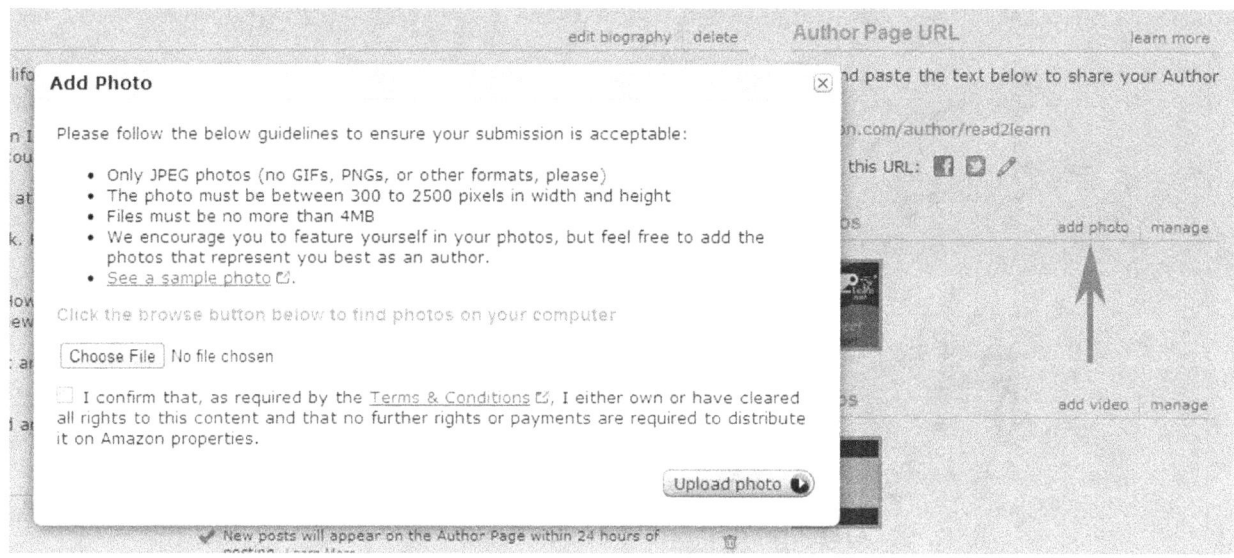

Figure 45

Below this section is an area for you to **upload videos**. If you recall earlier, I suggested that you make a promotional video using Animoto and to upload it to YouTube. If you followed those steps, then this section will be a breeze! It's actually a 2 step process, but it's not hard.

First you need to sign into your Animoto account, download the video you created in High Definition, and then save it to your desktop. The video you download from Animoto is in MP4 format, but Amazon will only accept video files that are avi, flv, mov, mpg, and wmv. I'm not sure if a "mpg" file and MP4 are the same, so I'll show you how to convert it to a WMV file.

To convert your video file to WMV, open your video using **Windows Live Movie Maker**. Windows Movie Maker will <u>automatically</u> re-format your video into a WMV file. When the video is finished formatting, navigate to the top right corner, click the "*Save Movie*" button, and choose the "*For computer*" option. (*Figure 46.*)

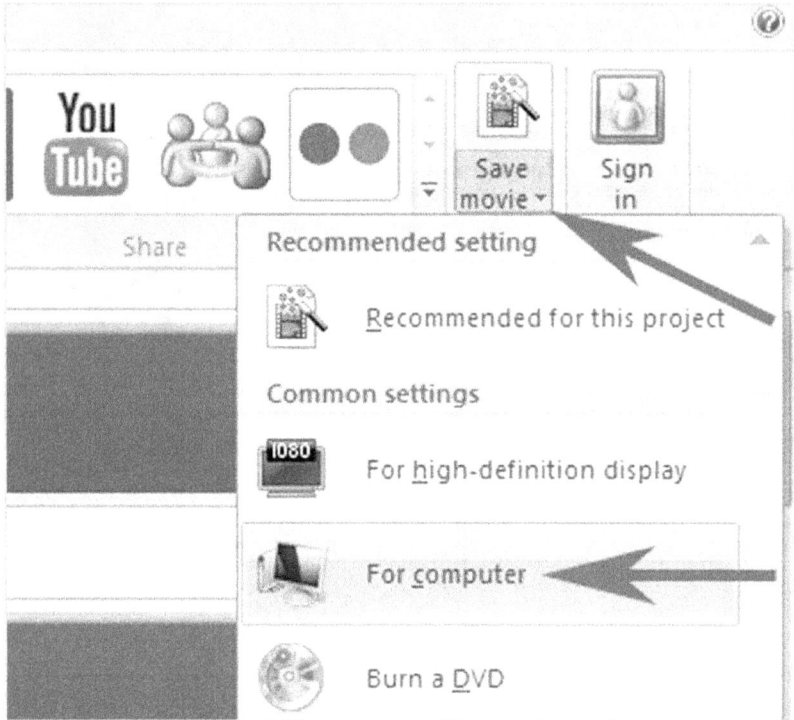

Figure 46

It might take 5–15 minutes for your video to save depending on how long it is. When it's complete, you'll have a **perfect WMV video file** to upload to Amazon. When you attempt to upload your video to Amazon, it might **not work** the first couple times. I think it actually took me about 10 or 15 times before my video finally uploaded. So if you run into this same problem, just relax and try again later. (*Figure 47.*)

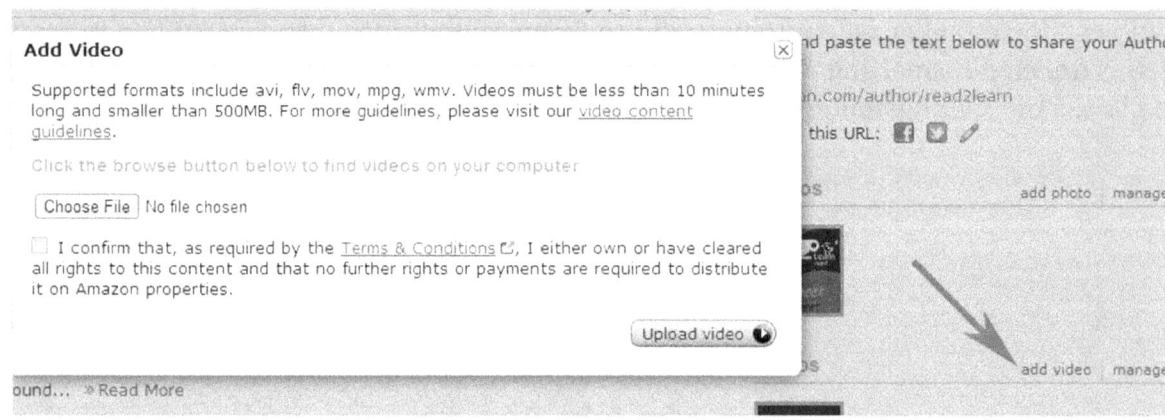

Figure 47

Next you'll see a section for your **Twitter** account. This is another reason why I told you to create a Twitter account earlier. Just enter your Twitter username, and Amazon will show your most recent "Tweet" on your profile page. (*Figure 48.*)

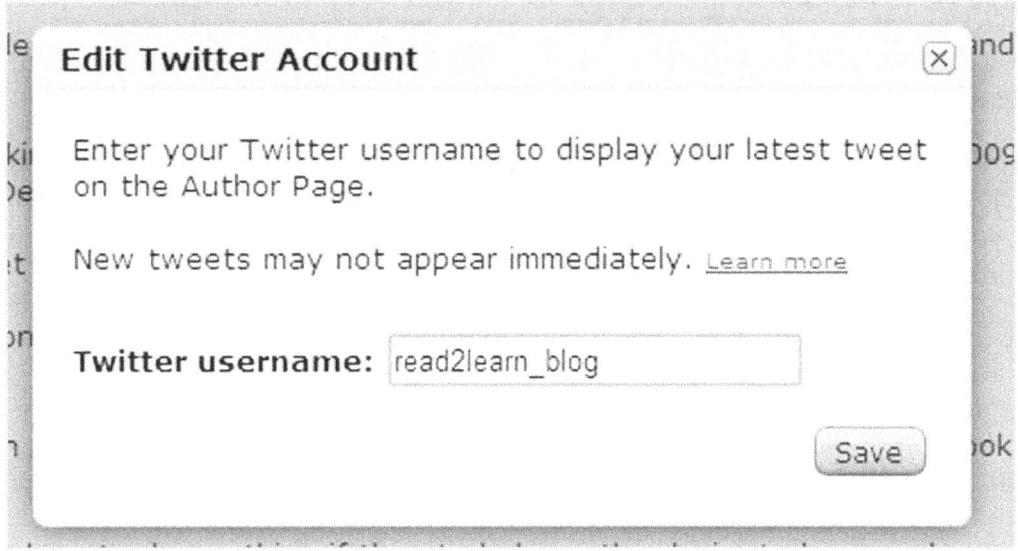

Figure 48

If you use Twitter like a normal human being, then it'll allow people to see what you're up too for the day. If somebody visits your Amazon profile and they look at your Twitter update, which Twitter update do **you** think looks best?

1. "Buy my new book!!! – www.amazon.com/link "
2. "My book is on sale for 99 cents! Go get it now! – www.amazon/link"
3. "I'm eating the best ice-cream right now. Mint chocolate chip!"

Obviously #3 is the best choice. If someone's on your Amazon profile, then they're already thinking about buying your book. They're just looking at your profile to learn more about you because they have no idea who you are. So give people a chance to learn more about you before you scream at them to *buy your book now!!*" in a Twitter update. (*Figure 49.*)

Figure 49

A potential reader might like mint chocolate chip ice-cream too and buy your book. Being a "real" person goes a long way in a cyber world filled with advertisements and spam.

Now I want to direct your attention back to the "tabs" along the top of Author Central. There are a few new tabs that I want to go cover.

The "**Sales Info**" tab only applies to paperback books. If you turned your kindle book into a paperback book, then you can check your sales info on this page. If you want to check your sales for your kindle eBook, then log back into your Kindle Direct Publishing Dashboard or use this link: http://kdp.amazon.com/mn/reports.

The next tab along the top says "**Customer Reviews**." This is where you can see all the reviews for your *all* your books. The next tab along the top says "**Help.**" So if you need additional help with Author Central, click the "help" tab to find a solution to your problem.

<u>Important Update</u>: Amazon has added a new tab that says "Rank." Amazon Author Rank is based on the sales of <u>all of your books</u> on Amazon.com and is updated hourly. (*Figure 50.*)

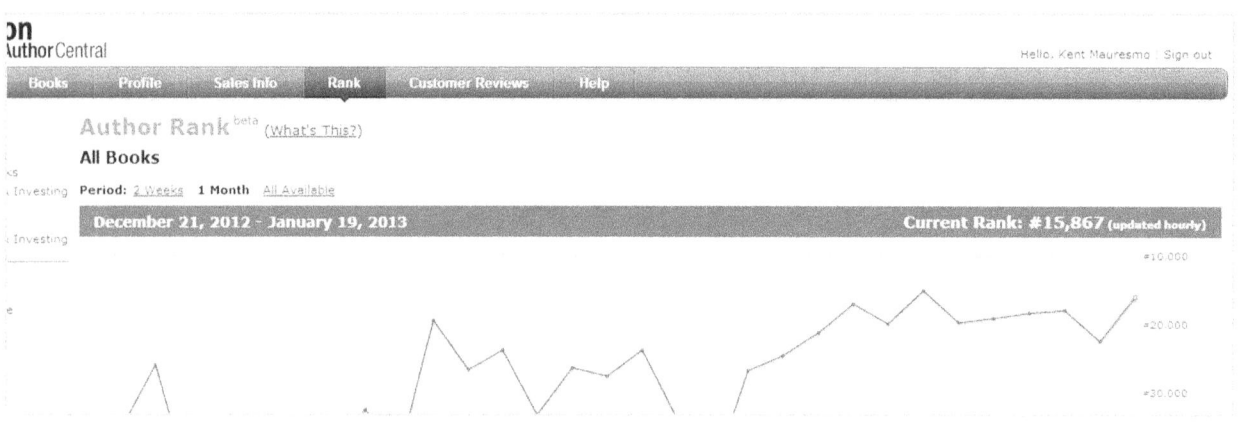

Figure 50

I was about to move on to the next chapter in this book, but I just noticed something very interesting about Author Central. I just clicked the "**Books**" tab, clicked on one of my books, and a page opened that I've never seen before.

On this page you can add *Editorial Reviews*, and update your books description using **bullet points**, **bold font**, and **italics**. (*Figure 51.*) There's also a section that says "*From the Author*" where you can add an additional comment and/or notation. And finally, there's an "*About the Author*" section where you can add more information about yourself to compliment your biography.

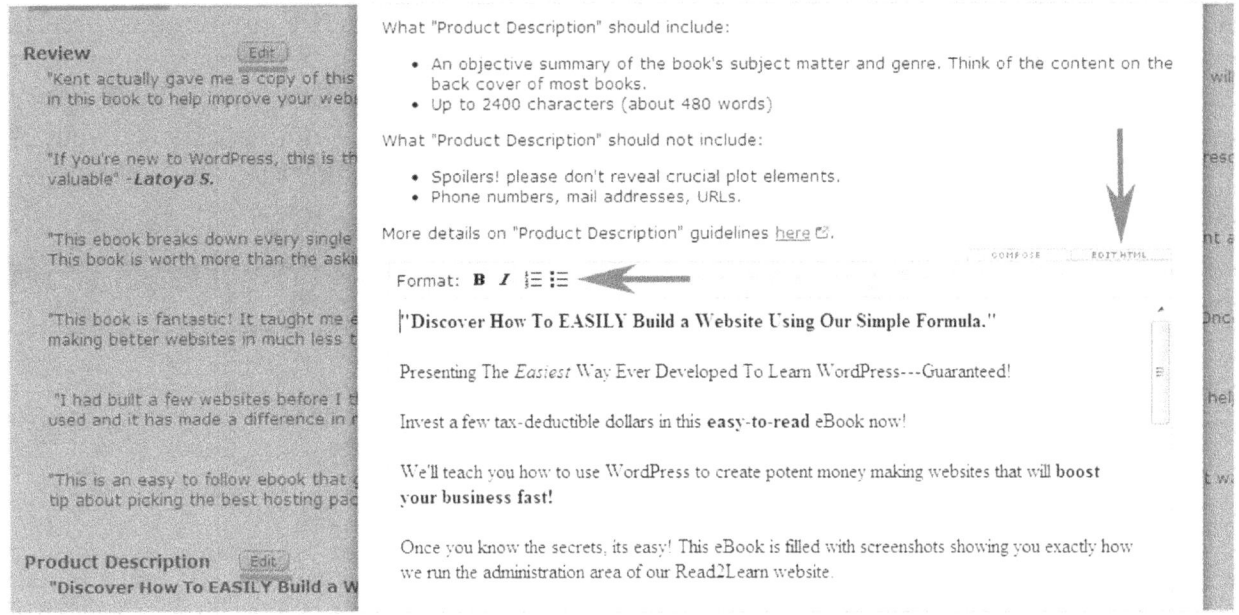

Figure 51

You can format all these sections using bold font, italics, or bullet points. There's also an **EDIT HTML** tab that you can click. If you click this tab, you can enter in custom HTML code to make your products page look more dynamic. I always wondered how people were doing that, and I now I know.

You can also click the "**Book Details**" tab if you want to view some basic information about your book. Next to that is a tab that says "**Book Extras**." This section encourages you to sign up for a website called Shelfari. Shelfari will all allow readers to see "*Book Extras*" for your book on the Kindle and Kindle apps for iPad, iPhone, and iPod Touch. The website is **http://www.shelfari.com** which is another site by Amazon. (*Figure 52.*)

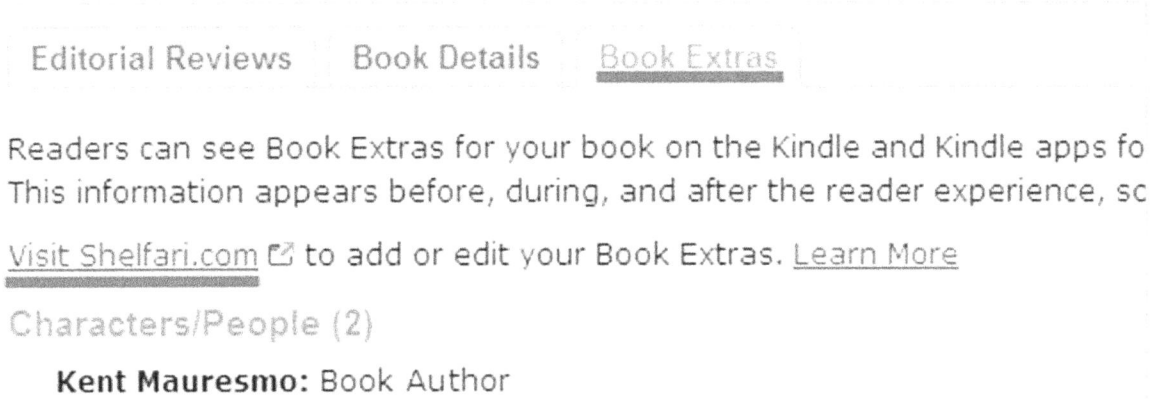

Figure 52

Shelfari is like Wikipedia for Amazon books. **Shelfari users can edit your books profile page** to add/edit your books description, simplified synopsis, summary, etc. If you're using Shelfari for the first time, you will notice that only your books description is filled out. If you click the *"read more..."* button under your description, you'll notice that your books description might be a jumbled mess or just empty. You need to click the "edit" tab and fix this immediately. (*Figure 53.*)

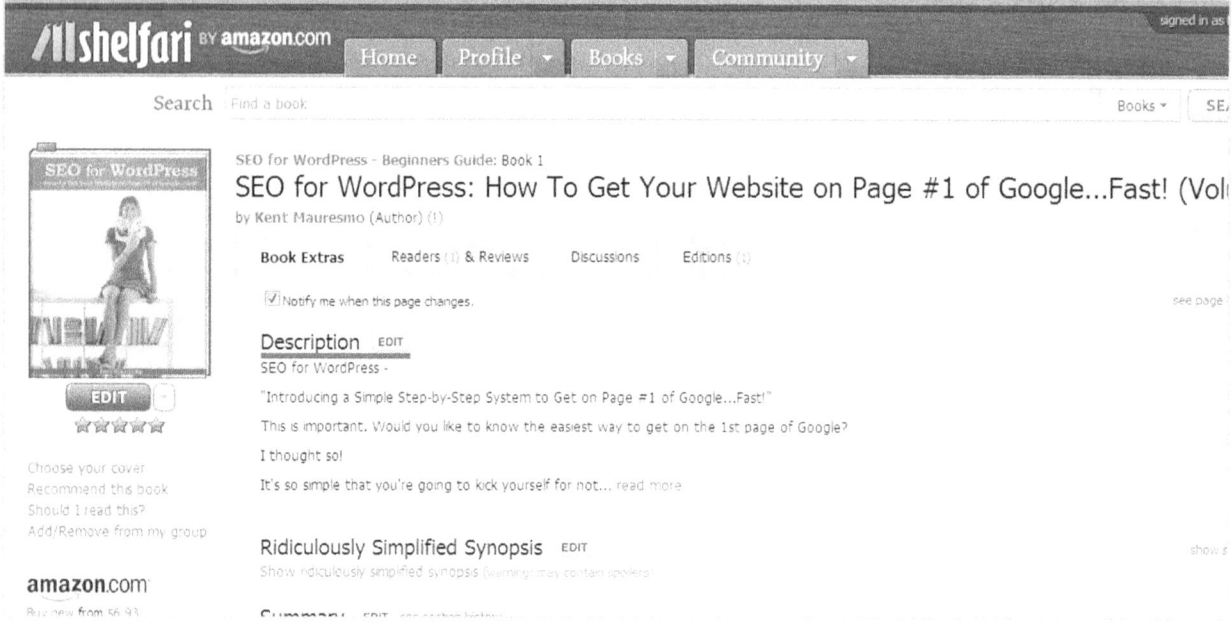

Figure 53

Next, scroll down the page and **start filling out the profile page yourself**. There's a 90% chance that the rest of your books profile page will be blank because no one has added any information there. Remember, it's like Wikipedia and so it's up to Shelfari users to create this page.

You should try to fill out this entire page if you can, but the most important areas are:

- Description
- Authors & Contributors
- Links to Supplemental Material
- More Books Like This

The "**Links to Supplemental Material**" lets you add a link to your website. So once again, your website comes in handy. (*Figure 54.*)

Links to Supplemental Material

Link to external websites where users can learn more about this book. (see instructions and examples)

Order | Name of website
1 | Read2Lean Blog

Link to webpage (URL)
http://read2learn.net

Description of webpage or website (optional)
Small Business Marketing Blog

Figure 54

The "**More Books Like This**" link is very important. You can use this section to search for books that are similar to yours, and add them on your profile. Obviously, you should **find the #1 bestselling book in your category and add that to your profile page**. If you've written other books that are within the same genre, then you should also search for those books and add them to this page as well. (*Figure 55.*)

Figure 55

Last but not lease, scroll back up to the top of the page and you'll see a **drop down list** that you can click under your book. Check the box that says "**I've read it**", click the **heart icon** to favorite the book, and click the **vault icon** to publicly display that you own the book. Finally underneath the drop down menu, you'll see **5 stars** which you can click on. Give your book a 5 star rating because you're awesome! (*Figure 56.*)

Figure 56

Make sure that you rate and add other books that you've read too. If someone clicks your profile and see that you only rated/added your own book, it will look like self promotion. If you do decide to rate other books, only rate the books that you really like so you can give out a legit 5 star rating. **Don't ever rate another indie author with a 1 star rating** because he will just turn around and do the same thing to you.

If you don't like a book that you've read from another indie author, you need to keep it to yourself. **Don't ever** publicly shame someone else's book on Shelfari and/or Amazon if you're a book author yourself. It doesn't matter if they're selling more copies than you and you think your book is better. That's unprofessional and bad karma. Instead, why not contact them and ask them for some tips if they're selling a lot of books. They might help you out.

Once you're done, you should see something that says "**Book Extras from the Shelfari Community**" on your Amazons product page. It should be right above the *"More About the Author"* section towards the bottom. It might take 12 hours to show up, so be patient. (*Figure 57.*)

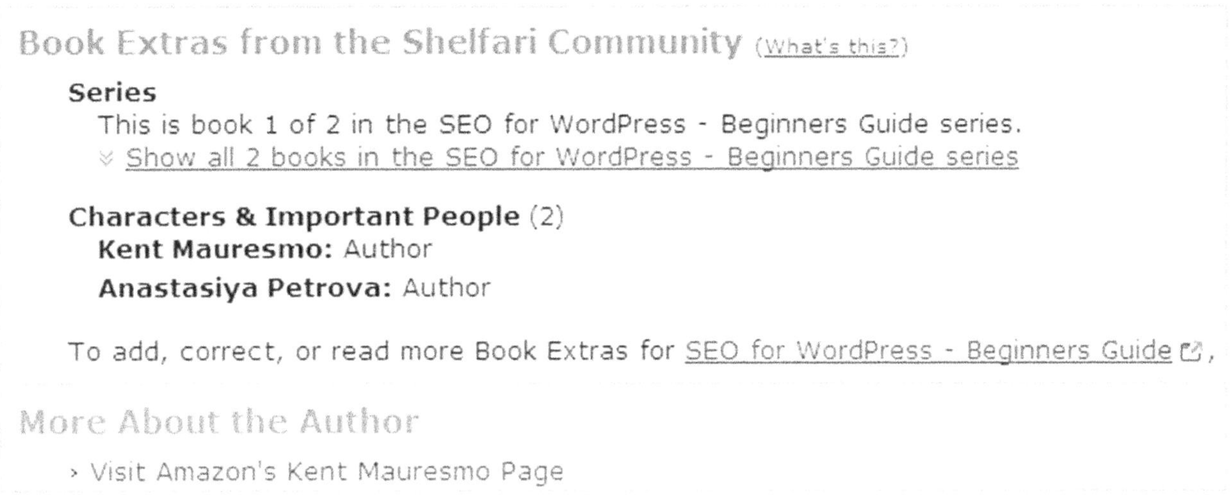

Book Extras from the Shelfari Community (What's this?)

Series
This is book 1 of 2 in the SEO for WordPress - Beginners Guide series.
⌄ Show all 2 books in the SEO for WordPress - Beginners Guide series

Characters & Important People (2)
Kent Mauresmo: Author
Anastasiya Petrova: Author

To add, correct, or read more Book Extras for SEO for WordPress - Beginners Guide ⌐,

More About the Author

› Visit Amazon's Kent Mauresmo Page

Figure 57

Keep in mind that you have to wait for Amazon to verify and add your books to your Author Central account **first**. After Amazon adds your book to your Author Central account, then you can click on your book titles within the "**Books**" tab and customize your pages.

I can't believe I missed all this before. I just found out about HTML formatting and Shelfari as I was writing this book. Good thing I wrote this book then!

The reason I'm being upfront about this is because my books sell pretty good and I've missed all those steps. So now you're **ahead of the game**, and you'll most likely sell more books than me.

Chapter 7

How to Use Your Website/Blog to Promote Your eBook

The first thing you should do is add your eBook to the **sidebar** on your website. When someone clicks on your book, you want that person to be redirected to your Amazon product page. I found a very easy way to do this if you're running your website using the WordPress platform.

WordPress has a widget that's called "**Image Jetpack**" (*Figure 58.*) This widget will ask you for the "Image URL" which means that you need to host your image. So the first thing you need to do is resize your eBook cover image so it'll fit nicely on your sidebar. You can resize your image using *Windows Photo Gallery*, *Photoshop*, or a *Paint* program.

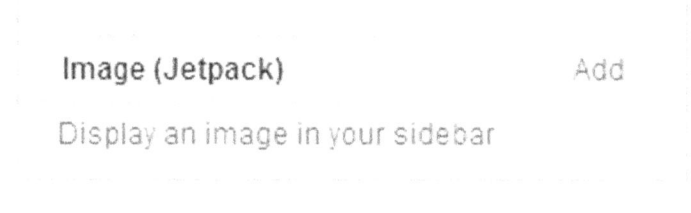

Figure 58

Next you need to host your resized image because you need the "Image URL." You can host the image using the "Media" tab within your WordPress Dashboard, or you can upload the image using a website like Photobucket. After you upload the image, both WordPress and Photobucket will give you a **File URL** address that directly links to the image. (*Figure 59.*) You need to copy and paste that URL into the "Image URL" section of the widget.

Figure 59

For the "Image Alignment" section, select "Center" from the drop down box. Below that you'll see another section that says "Width and Height." Enter the same width and height that you used to resize the image. If you leave these fields blank, then the widget will attempt to guess the image size, and your image may show up blurry on your website.

If you don't know what your image dimensions are, then *right click* on your image, click *properties*, and then click the *details* tab. There you will find the Height and Width for your image. (*Figure 60*.)

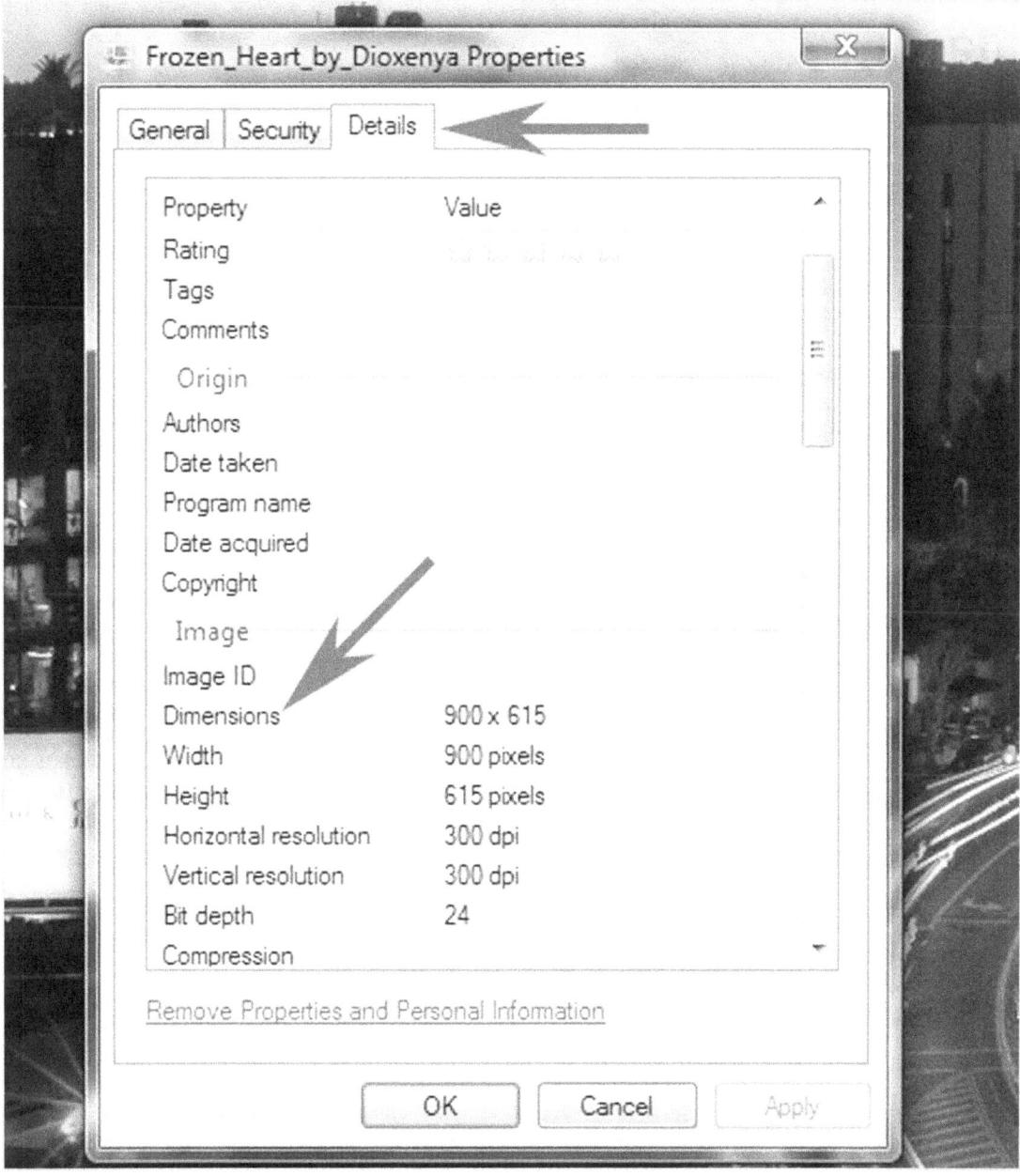

Figure 60

Lastly, you'll need to enter in your "Link URL" which will redirect people when they click on your image. This is where you need to enter the URL for your **Amazon Products Page**.

To find your "Link URL", go to Amazon, find your products page for your book, and <u>copy the web address displayed in the URL area</u>. Then click back over to WordPress, and paste the URL into the "Link URL" box. (*Figure 61.*)

Figure 61

There are a few more areas to fill out on this widget too, but they're common sense. You can enter a widget title, alternate text, image title, and a caption for your image. (*Figure 62.*)

Figure 62

After you fill in all these areas, save your widget to see what it looks like on your website. (*Figure 63.*)

"How To Build a Website With
WordPress" - 2nd Edition eBook

Figure 63

Shelfari also has a custom widget that you can add to your website. Sign into Shelfari, click the *Profile* tab, and then click the drop down menu on the *"more"* tab. At the very bottom, you'll see an option that says "**My Widgets**." (*Figure 64.*)

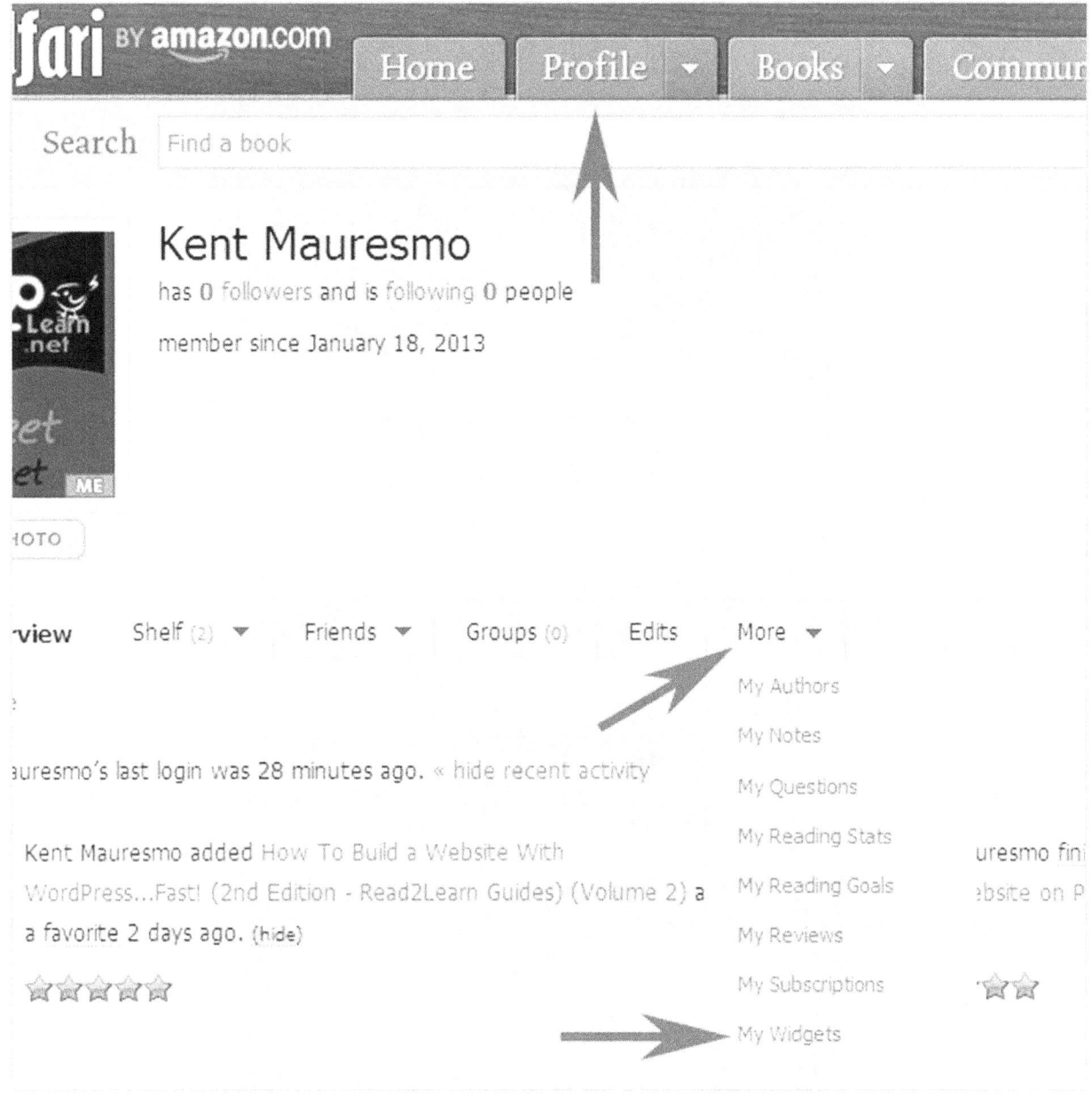

Figure 64

Next you'll have to choose if you have a WordPress website or Blogger account. Choose WordPress, and then you can start to customize your **bookshelf style widget**. (*Figure 65.*) When you're done creating your widget, Shelfari will give you some HTML code to post on your websites sidebar. If you're familiar with WordPress, then you know that you can enter HTML code into your "text" widgets.

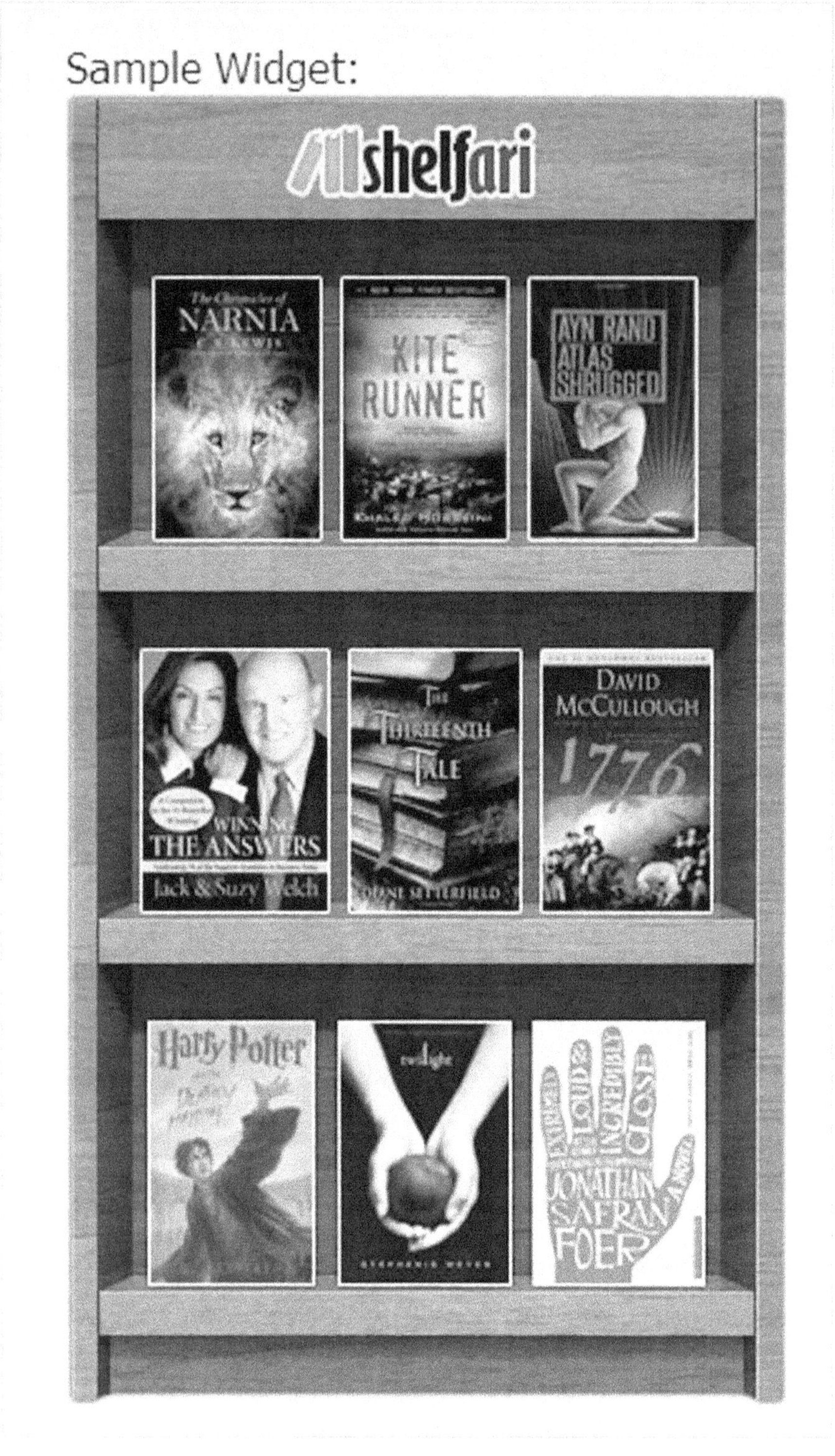
Sample Widget:
shelfari
The Chronicles of
NARNIA
KITE
RUNNER
AYN RAND
ATLAS
SHRUGGED
WINNING
THE ANSWERS
Jack & Suzy Welch
THE
THIRTEENTH
TALE
DAVID
McCULLOUGH
1776
Harry Potter
twilight
JONATHAN
SAFRAN
FOER

Figure 65

How to Start an Email List

I recommend that you sign up with *Aweber* to take care of all your email marketing. There are other companies that you can use too, but Aweber has great customer service and a toll free number to call if you need help. Their website is **www.aweber.com**.

I'm not going to walk you through the entire Aweber process because that's beyond the scope of this book. Instead, I'll give you a few pointers to save you time and help you avoid unnecessary headaches.

As you're setting up your email list, Aweber will ask you what type of form you want to use. Select the form that says "**Light Box**." A light box form will "pop-up" when someone visits your website and black-out the background. This has been proven to increase email sign-ups, so I recommend that you use this feature. (*Figure 66.*)

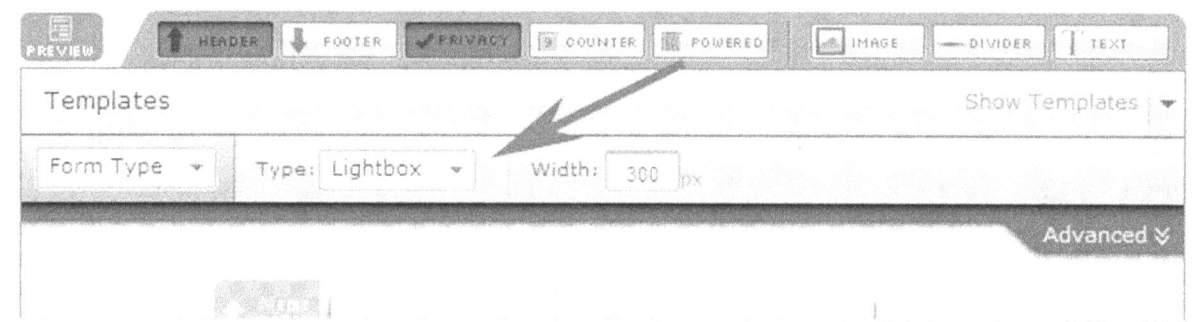

Figure 66

Next you want to click the "**Advanced**" drop down tab where you'll see additional options. For the display option select "**Fade In**", and for the delay option you can enter 1-3 seconds. I wouldn't select anything longer than 3 seconds.

You want your light box to appear **before** people starting reading the articles on your website. If your light box pops up while people are reading, then they'll probably close it out very quickly without even looking at it because you're interrupting them.

The next option you'll see is something that says "**Recurrence**." By default, I believe its set to "Always Display", but that is not the best option. The "Always Display" option will show your light box **every time** someone navigates to a new page on your website. That will drive people crazy and they'll leave your website almost immediately.

Instead, click the drop down menu, and select the option that says "**Show Every X Days**", and for the *day's* options select **1 or 2**. This option will show your light box only *once* per day to the same person which is better. (*Figure 67.*)

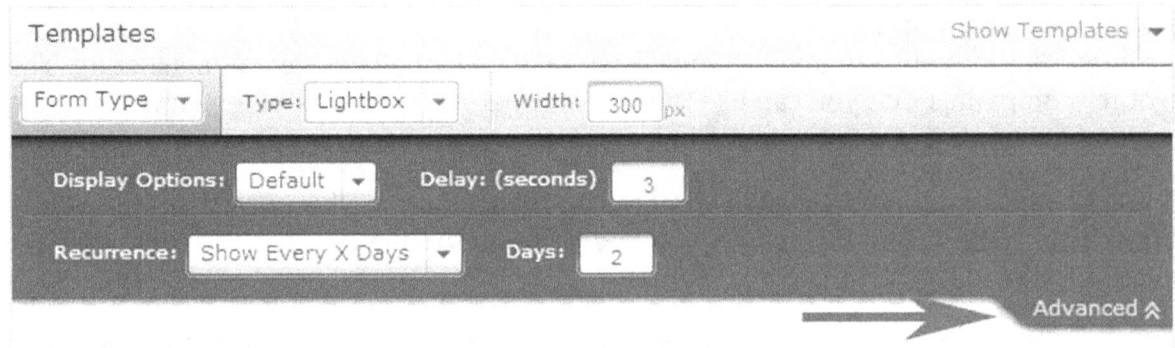

Figure 67

Next you want to create an additional webform for the same list which is called an "**Inline**" form. This is a form that you can add to your sidebar which isn't intrusive like the light box.

As for the text in your lightbox, I encourage you to **offer free chapters of your eBook** in exchange for their email address. I showed you earlier how to turn your eBook into a PDF document, so PDF the first 3 or 4 chapters of your eBook and give them away for **FREE**! (*Figure 68.*)

Welcome To Read2Learn.net!

Newest Book: "Amazon Kindle Marketing Strategy Guide!"

<u>Sign up now</u> to download the first 4 chapters for *FREE*!

Name:

Email:

SUBMIT

We respect your

Figure 68

To upload your sample PDF document to WordPress, just use the *Media* tab within your WordPress dashboard. After you upload the sample of your eBook, WordPress will give you a file URL that links to the PDF document.

Next create a new page on your website that will be your download page. On this page you can write some text, include your books image, and add the **link to your PDF document**. (*Figure 69.*)

SAMPLE EBOOK

Click to Download Now! —-> E-Book Marketing: How To Publish and Market Your E-Books For Amazon (First 2 Chapters)

Figure 69

There's a 90% chance that WordPress will automatically display your ebook download page on your websites navigation menu. That's not good because **you want this download page to be hidden.**

To hide the page within WordPress, click the "*Appearance*" tab, then "*Menus*", and find the download page that you just created. Click the drop down arrow on your download page, and select the "*Remove*" option. This doesn't delete the page; it just removes it from the main navigation menu on your website. Now the page is hidden.

Next you need to sign back into your Aweber account. When you're setting up your list with Aweber, they're going to ask you for a "**Confirmation Success Page URL**." This is a page on your website that people are redirected too after they confirm their email address. In this section, you should **enter the link to your hidden download page**. (*Figure 70.*)

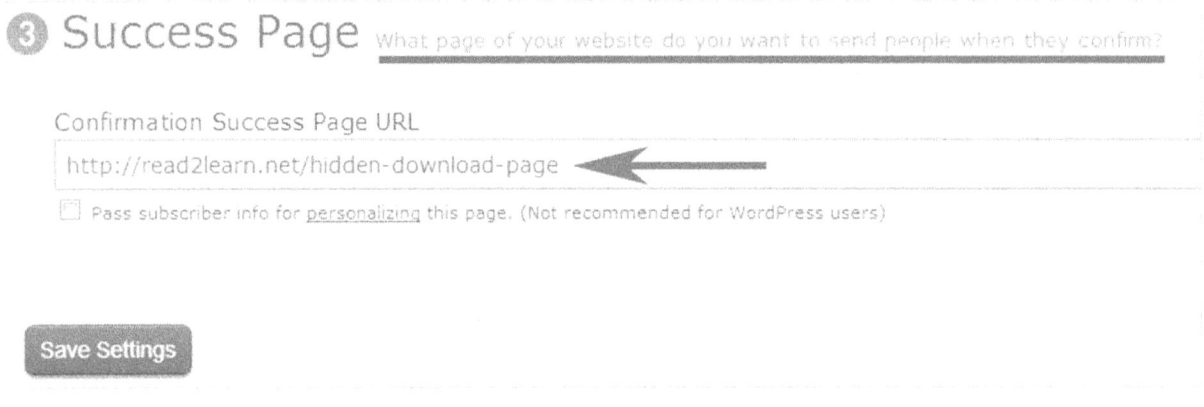

Figure 70

Now every time somebody signs up for your email list, they'll be **automatically redirected** to your hidden page where they can download the sample of your book. If your book is amazing, then people shouldn't have a problem paying $2.99-$4.99 to read the rest of your book.

You can also set up follow up messages with Aweber. If you **send out 1 message per week**, that's usually good! You want people to remember you, but you don't want to overwhelm them with too many emails or they'll unsubscribe.

If you don't know what to write in your follow up emails, **don't panic**. You can write really short emails asking your subscribers to check out your latest blog posts. As a book author, what should you blog about?

How to Write Effective Blog Posts
If you're a non-fiction writer, then you can write blog posts to **fill in the blanks** from your book. For example, by now you should know that we have another book about building websites with *WordPress*.

There's no way I could include every single detail about building a website into a 121 page Kindle book. That would require a 500 page book which most people wouldn't even read.

Instead, I wait for readers to contact me with questions and I use those questions to give me ideas for blog posts. This helps me write useful posts that everybody can benefit from, and it also saves me time if someone else emails me with the same question. Instead of typing out the same answer twice, I can send them a link to our blog post that will answer their question. (*Figure 71.*)

HOW TO DISABLE COMMENTS ON WORDPRESS PAGES

by KENT MAURESMO on DECEMBER 13, 2012 in HOW TO DISABLE COMMENTS ON WORDPRESS PAGES, MARKETING with 5 COMMENTS *[edit]*

Tweet 10

HOW TO DISABLE COMMENTS ON WORDPRESS PAGES AND POSTS

I received a few emails asking me how to disable the comments on WordPress pages. For example, you

Figure 71

At the end of *some* of your blog posts, you can **include a link to your Amazons product page**. I recommend that you use an image of your book along with a *"Checkout with Amazon"* button. If someone finds your blog post by searching via Google, they will see that you have a book available on Amazon with more information. (*Figure 72.*)

transform WordPress into a beautiful fully functional website. Just grab our book on Amazon for more details because this article is already long enough! 😄

How To Build a Website With WordPress

Figure 72

The reason that I recommend using an Amazon button is because people are familiar with Amazon and they **trust** them as a vendor. All you have to do is link the Amazon button to your products page where people can purchase your book.

To find an Amazon button, just type "**Amazon Buttons**" into Google and then click the "Images" tab to search Google Images. You should see plenty of Amazon buttons that you can use for your website.

Don't worry about copyright infringement because 95% of those buttons are offered on Amazons website for **free**. Here's the link to the Amazons "buttons" page if you'd prefer to be 100% safe: https://payments.amazon.com/sdui/sdui/helpTab/Checkout-by-Amazon/Integrating-with-Checkout-by-Amazon/Choosing-Buttons-for-Your-Website (*Figure 73.*)

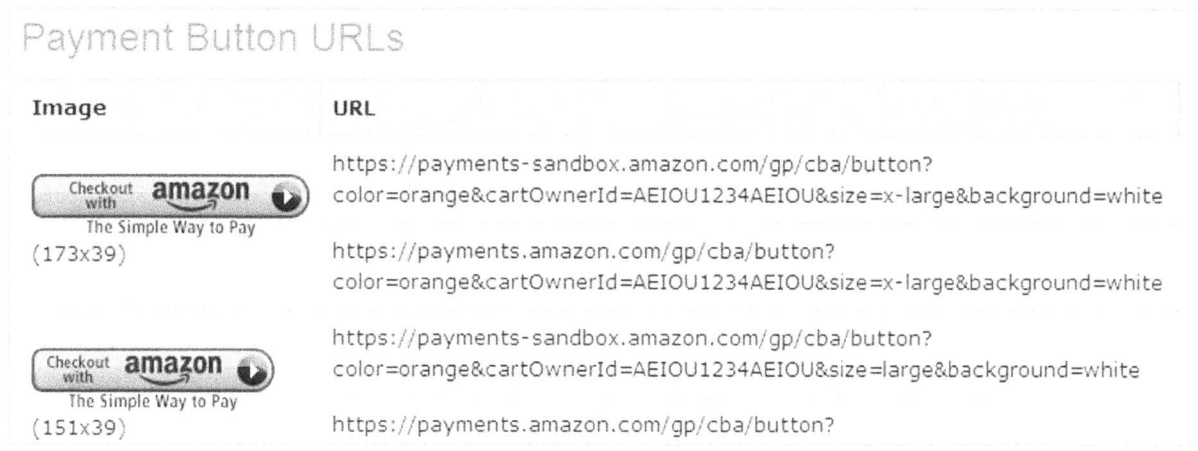

Figure 73

To link the button to your Amazons page, just highlight the button, click the hyperlink icon on your WordPress toolbar, and then enter in the URL to your products page. Now when people click on the button, they'll automatically be redirected to your products page to buy your book.

If you're a **fiction writer**, then you need to be more creative with your blog posts. Since I'm not a fiction writer, I can only give you a few ideas that I personally think are interesting and that would grab my attention.

I think it would be really creative if you wrote a blog **post for each character** in your book. It could be like a biography or some type of back-story for each character that's not even mentioned in your book. This would give your characters more depth and make them more interesting.

Keep in mind that you've syndicated your blog posts to your *Author Central* profile using the RSS feed. So now when someone visits your Author Central profile, they'll see your most recent blog posts describing the characters in your book. That's 100% better than a blog post that says *"Hi! My new romance novel is available….buy it now on Amazon!!!!"*

If you only plan to write "self-promoting" blog posts *endlessly* advertising your book, then don't even bother uploading your RSS feed to your Author Central account.

Imagine how it looks if someone views your Author Central profile and your **Biography**, **Tweets**, and **RSS Feed** says, "*Buy my book today!! It's available on Amazon!*" The person is already on Amazon, and they can see that your book is available. So you're just stating the obvious instead of writing something that compliments your book.

Give people a <u>reason</u> to buy your book instead of just telling them to buy it. Give them a <u>reason</u> to want click on your Twitter profile and connect with you. Give them a <u>reason</u> to click on your RSS feed to read your entire blog posts.

If you're a fiction writer, than you already have a pretty good imagination. Put some of that creativity to use and hook people in with your characters. Write your blog posts as if the characters are writing it. Create multiple authors on your website using the main characters in your book.

Try to make your characters come to life as if they're real people. You can even **comment your own blog post using your characters names too**. Turn your fantasy world into a real world. If people like your book, they will probably visit your website often to "talk" with the characters in your book. Some people are weird like that, and they like to role play with the characters in the book. Take advantage of that and have fun.

If you're a fiction writer, you shouldn't even write a blog saying *"BUY MY BOOK."* People already know you're a book author because they can see your book on the sidebar of your website. They're most likely **visiting your website to check out your writing style**, or to see what you're blogging about.

Fiction and **Non-Fiction** books are two different animals. When people buy non-fiction books, it's because they're trying to learn something new. But when people buy **Fiction** books, it's because they're bored or need be entertained. So entertain your readers! You have the *"green light"* to be exciting, <u>bold</u>, <u>risky</u>, and <u>politically incorrect</u>.

<u>Fiction Writers:</u> If you write boring blog post, then people will probably think that your books are boring too. But if you write wild and entertaining blogs posts, then you'll probably peak someone's interest and they'll pay $2.99 and take a chance on your book.

Chapter 8

How to Get Book Reviews That Stick

Most people ask their friends and family to review their books on Amazon. There's absolutely nothing wrong with that, but you might run into a problem. So many people have abused the Amazon Review system that there's a 50% chance that Amazon will remove a review that's not an *"Amazon Verified Purchase"* review. (*Figure 74.*)

> ☆☆☆☆☆ **Excellent book**, January 10, 2013
>
> By **Mirella DeBoni** - See all my reviews
>
> Amazon Verified Purchase (What's this?)
> This review is from: SEO for WordPress: How To Get Your Website on Page #1

Figure 74

So don't bother telling your friends to review your book if they haven't downloaded it from Amazon. Their review might stick for a week or two, but there's a good chance that it'll get removed.

I had about 19 reviews on my book and now I only have 11. Amazon removed all the reviews from my friends and family PLUS about 5 legit reviews from people who bought the book.

You can still have your friend's review your book, but they need to buy it. If they're too cheap to buy it, then ask them to download it when you run a **free promo day** with KDP Select. When someone downloads your book for free and writes a review, it still shows up as an Amazon Verified Purchase review.

To run a free promotion you need to sign into your KDP dashboard. Next click the checkbox next to the book that you want to run the free promo for, and click the *"Actions"* drop down menu. The last item on that menu says "**Manage Promotions**" and that's where you can set up a free promo day. (*Figure 75.*)

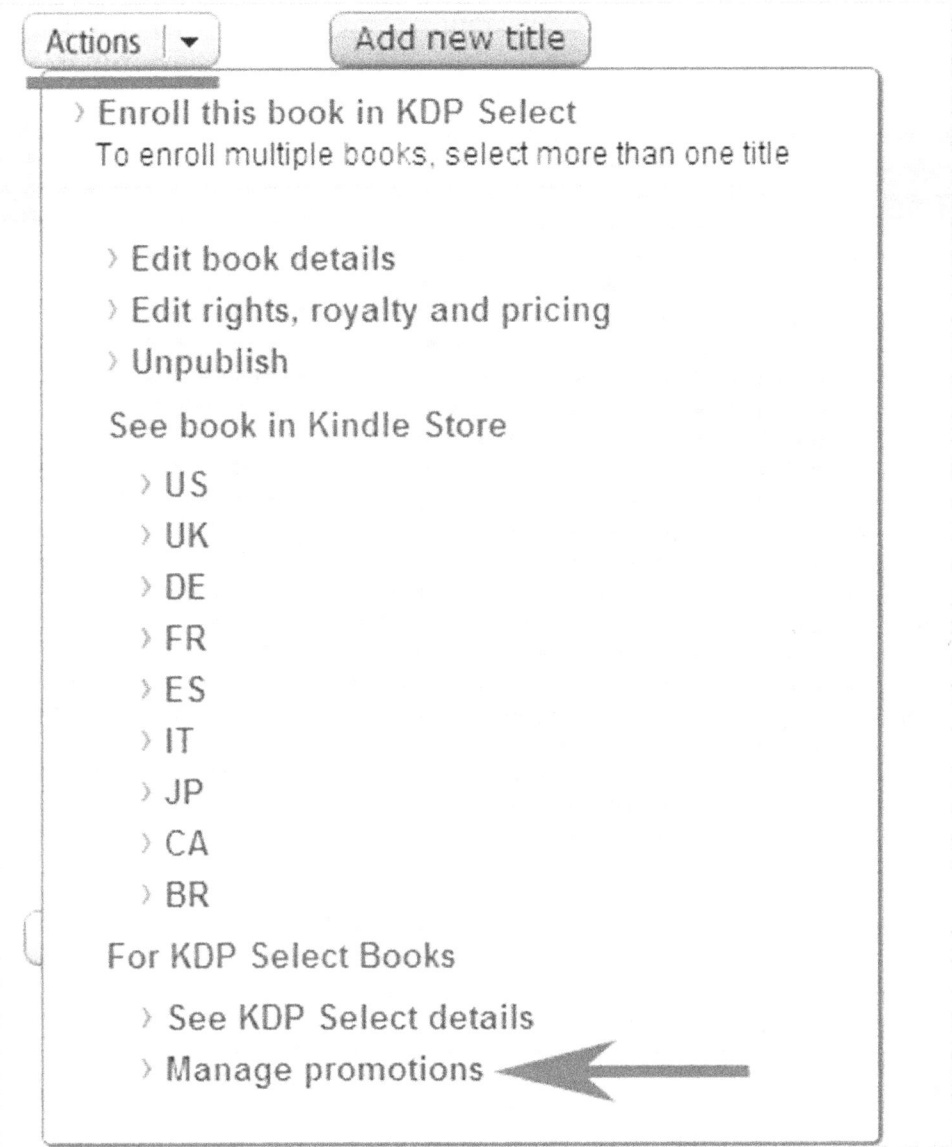

Figure 75

You need to use your free promo days wisely because you only have 5 to use within a 90 day period. So I suggest that you **plan 3 or 4 days ahead** before you run a fee promotional day. You should even write a blog post stating which day your book will be available for free. People like FREE stuff! New visitors to your website might sign up to your email list too because you're giving them a heads up on the free promo day.

Next you need to send out a broadcast email (using Aweber) letting your subscribers know which day they can download your book for free. Some people on your email list will only have the sample PDF copy of your book. They'll be happy to know they can download the rest of the book for **FREE**.

All you have to do now is wait a few days, and then ask your friends to go review your book. Some of your friends will promise to write the review and never do it. Some of your other friends will forget to download your book on the free promo day, so even if they write a review it's useless. I'm just giving you a heads up on what to expect because everything doesn't **always** work out like you plan.

You'll also get some emails from people saying something like, "_Thank you for the free book! I can't wait to read it!_" Make sure that you respond to those emails and ask them to give your book a good review if they like it. Make sure to **include a direct link to the review page** on Amazon within your email. Some people will be so happy that you gave them a free book that they'll review your book the same day.

Lastly, send out a broadcast email to your list asking them to review your book if they liked it. Here's an example of an email that you can send out and/or add to your follow up emails:

"Hello friends!

We would like to thank everybody for the kind words about our eBook,"**[Enter eBook Title Here.]**_" I know you're busy, but if you could spare 30 seconds, could you please **post a _quick_ review on Amazon for us**? **You could write just 2 sentences** to let other potential readers know why you liked our eBook._

Please do this for us because it will be greatly appreciated! Here's a link to the review page:

http://www.amazon.com/Your-eBook-Here /product-reviews/B007BJ2902/

**Thank you** so much for your support! Email me after you post the review, and I'll send you a bonus eBook for **FREE**."

As you noticed, it might be a good idea to offer an incentive for book reviews. You can offer another bonus eBook, a short article, a preview to your new book, a free iPod....just kidding about the iPod. Ha-ha.

The Truth About Book Reviews

Even after all this, some people still won't review your book even if they love it. I get a couple emails per day from people that say they really liked our eBooks. I ask them if they can copy and paste exactly what they said in their email and post it on Amazon, and they all say "Okay!!" I check Amazon a few days later and **NOTHING**!

Don't worry about it too much. If people really like your book, then they'll spread the word about it and that's 100 times better than a review. I noticed that most people were emailing me from their mobile phone which makes a huge difference.

It takes about 2 minutes to post a review on Amazon using a computer, but it would take about **10 minutes to post a review using a mobile phone**. Combine that with text message alerts, Facebook notifications, and Twitter updates; the person never gets around to reviewing anything.

You only need about 4 or 5 *Amazon Verified Purchased* reviews and you're good. But if you pay people to give you **fake reviews**, you could hurt yourself in the end. For example, if you release a **new book** and within a week you magically have 20 Five Star reviews but a seller's rank of 317,000, then game over. Either Amazon is lying about your sellers rank, or your reviews are faked. Which do you think people will believe?

Also buying reviews is against Amazons terms of service, and you can get your account terminated. I don't know if they'll actually terminate your account, but it's not worth the risk.

If you decide to pay a close friend $5 to give him motivation to review your book right on the spot, then that's not a big deal. But if you **unknowingly** hire someone that's already on Amazon's radar for writing fraudulent reviews, then you're putting yourself at risk.

There's really no insiders secret to get **legit** book reviews. The absolute best way is to ask friends and family first so you can have 4-5 reviews on Amazon. After that, just connect with your readers via email and ask them.

We're just indie authors, so we **shouldn't expect to get 200 book reviews** because it's not realistic. New York Times Bestselling Authors sell about a million books (if not more) and they only have about 2000-3000 reviews. That means that less than 1% of the people that bought the book wrote a review for it.

So if less than 1% of the people that bought your indie book write a review, how many do you expect to get?! If you get over 10 **REAL** positive book reviews, that's really good! That means that people like you, so keep up the good work.

Updated Tip: You can give away free copies of your PDF book and ask people to leave an honest review on Amazon. What's the catch? They **must disclose** that the book was given to them for FREE, and Amazon will not delete the review.

Chapter 9

Other Things You Can Do on Amazon

You'll notice that Amazon has a "**Like**" button on your products page. You need to ask people to click your "Like" button because it's social proof that other people like your book. (*Figure 76.*)

Once again, there are only 3 legit ways to do this:

1. Send out an email to your list asking them to click the button.
2. Ask your close friends or family.
3. When someone sends you an email telling you how much they like your book, ask them if they could click the "Like" button on your page. Make sure to include a direct link to your product page to make it even easier for them. They might even leave you a review too since they're already on your page.

Figure 76

How To Use "Listmania"

People use Listmania Lists to add products they find interesting including books. You don't need to purchase these items from Amazon to add them to Listmania, so ask everybody you know if they can add your book to their Listmania list.

Depending on a person's search query, Listmania will display a **banner ad on the sidebar** with related books. For example, if you type "Crime Novels" into Amazons search bar, you'll notice 2 books on the left sidebar under the "Listmania!" section.

This is 100% free advertising for you! There's no guarantee that your book will show up in the sidebar, but it doesn't matter. You still need to take advantage of Listmania. (*Figure 77.*)

Figure 77

I know a lot of people that use the **search feature** on Amazon to browse through Listmania. If people are looking for romance novels, then they're probably going to type "romance novels" into the search bar when browsing through Listmania. (*Figure 78.*)

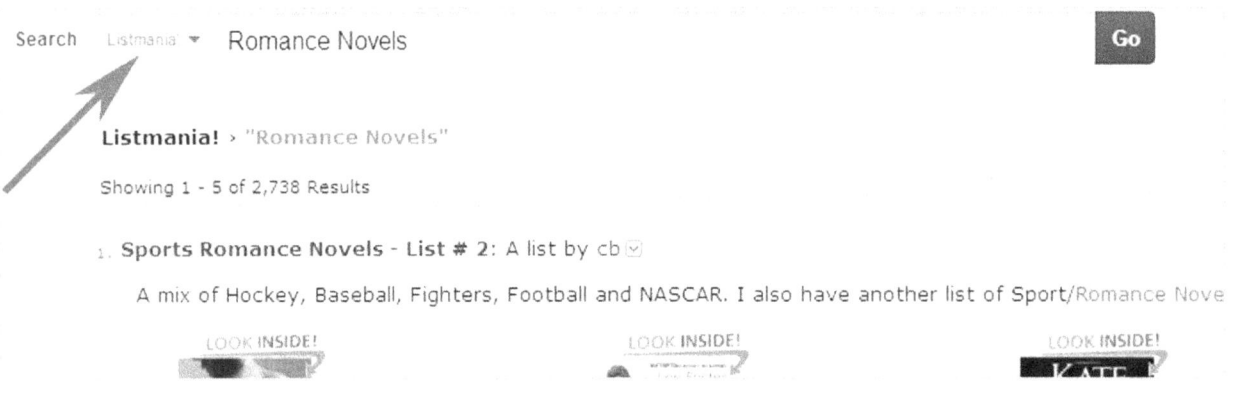

Figure 78

As mentioned earlier in this book, you can look through the "Tags" (if available) of other **New York Times Bestsellers** to see what keywords people are associating with certain books. After you do some research, you should create your own Listmania list.

To the **easiest** way to create a list is to follow the instructions via Amazon. So here's what you can do:

1. Visit your Amazon profile page (http://www.amazon.com/gp/pdp/profile/) and log into your account if requested.
2. Click the "Edit Your Profile" button on the top right-hand corner of the page.
3. Click the "Lists" tab in the Contributions section of Your Profile.
4. Click the "Create your first one now" link or "Manage your Listmania Lists" link if you already have existing lists.
5. Provide the requested information for your list and click the **Preview** button to review your list and **Publish list** when you are finished. (*See Figure 79.*)

Create a Listmania list

To create a Listmania list:

1. Visit your Profile page and log into your account if requested
2. Click the "Edit Your Profile" button on the top right-hand corner of the page.
3. Click the "Lists" tab in the Contributions section of Your Profile.
4. Click the "Create your first one now" link or "Manage your Listmania Lists" link if you already have existing lists.
5. Provide the requested information for your list and click the **Preview** button to review your list and **Publish list** when you are finished

Here's the information you'll be asked to enter:

- **Name Your List:** Enter a friendly title for your list
- **Your qualifications:** Your qualifications should be a description of why you're an expert in the subject of your list.
- **Introduction:** You can add an optional introductory paragraph to describe the list
- **Add a product:** This is the core of your list! You can add anything from the product listings on Amazon.com

Figure 79

You'll be redirected to a page that'll show you step by step how to create your own list. As you're creating your list, you'll notice you have the option to **name your list**, enter your **qualifications**, and an **introduction** for your list which is the description. (*Figure 80.*)

Figure 80

The way you name your list is very **important**. If you want people to actually find your list, then you need to enter your most important keywords into this field. Based on some quick research I performed on a NY Times Bestseller (*Fifty Shades of Grey*), the top tags for the book were "erotic romance" and "alpha male."

So if I had a similar book like *Fifty Shades of Grey*, I would create a Listmania List entitled "**Erotic Romance: Erotic Romance Books Featuring an Alpha Male.**" Next for my qualifications field, I would probably enter some text that says, "Erotic Romance Junkie." Finally in the introduction section, I would write something like:

"*Erotic Romance Books Featuring an Alpha Male (TOP 10): Check out my top 10 list of erotic romance novels. I love erotic romance, and I've read all these books multiple times. If you're an erotic romance fan like me, then you'll love these books. All these books feature a dominant alpha male...no whimps!*"

Now if you know anything about Search Engine Optimization (SEO), then you'll know exactly what I did. I titled my list using the main keyword first. Also in the introduction section, I used the phrase "**erotic romance**" four times, and it still doesn't read like spam.

If your title and introduction is relevant to someone's search query on listmania, then you'll leap frog everybody else and your list will move closer to page one. I'm 100% sure this works because I just did it about 10 minutes ago to see if it works. My list went from page 3 to page 1 for the term "*WordPress*" almost right away.

You'll notice that the keyword phrase you type into Amazon will show up **highlighted** within the listmania introduction/descriptions area. So listmania works similar to Google, and I'm pretty good with Google and SEO. (*Figure 81*.)

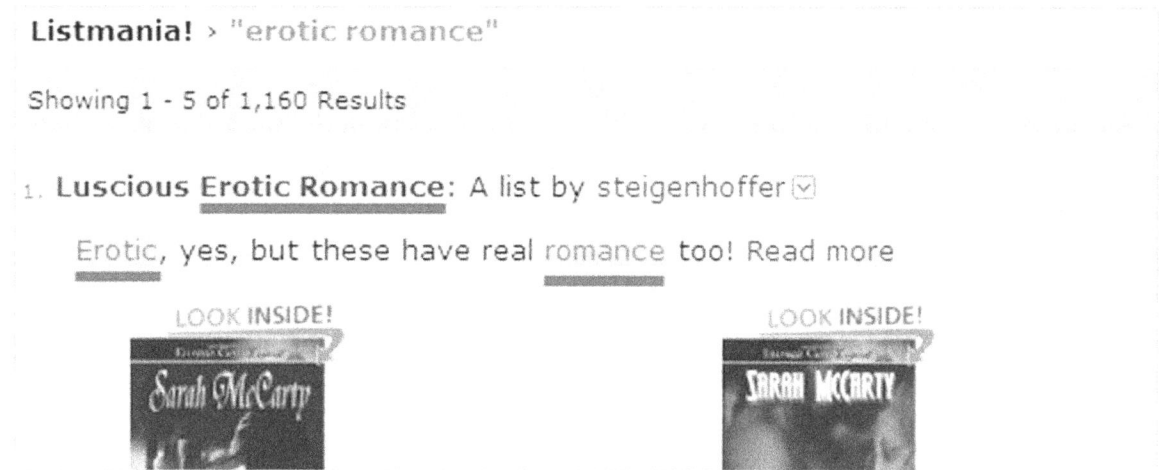

Figure 81

Please, **don't spam Listmania** and stuff keywords into the introduction/description area. You need to form your keywords together in a way that makes sense and reads well. You have to be very subtle with SEO or it'll backfire on you. If someone browsing through listmania figures out what you're doing, then you'll lose all credibility and they'll *think* you're a spammer.

Next you need to add your product to your listmania list. Click the orange button that says "**Add a product**", enter your books title, and click the "**go**" button. Click the "**select**" button next to your book and it'll be added to your list. Click the "**Add another**" button to add more books.

Make sure to add a few New York Times Bestselling authors on your list too. You want people to associate your book with other famous authors and their books. **Disclaimer:** It's a very bold move to claim your book is just as good as "*Fifty Shades of Grey*" or "*The Hunger Games.*" So make sure that your book can back up these claims or this strategy will backfire.

After you're done adding books to your list, click the "**preview**" button. If your list looks good, then click the "**Publish**" button and your Listmania List will go live. You can create multiple lists using Listmania, but don't abuse it. If people really like your book, then they'll add your book to their personal Listmania list without you even asking.

How To Add Tags (If available)
Near the bottom of your products page, you'll see a section that says "**Tags Customers Associate with This Product**." This is where people can check the boxes next to the tags they consider relevant to your book, or enter their own tags.

If you publish a <u>new</u> book on Amazon, then you won't have any tags for your book. So you can either wait for Amazon readers to enter tags, or <u>enter them yourself</u>. To enter your own tags, just enter a relevant keyword associated with your book into the "Your tags" box and click the "Add" button.

You can look at other bestselling books to see what tags their using, or just create your own. Since you're an indie author, you can even **enter your pen-name as a tag** and your websites name. (Your websites name, not your website address.)

I think there's been some misinformation passed on about the "tags" section on Amazon. If you pay someone to click your "erotic romance" tag 100 times from 100 different Amazon accounts, you're **not** going to magically appear on the first page of Amazon for the search term "erotic romance."

The search results displayed on Amazon are mainly based on the title of the book. You'd have a better chance of getting on page 1 for the search term "erotic romance" if your book was titled, "**Erotic Romance: An Erotic Story of Romance Gone Bad.**"

If someone clicks on your tags link (**the actual link**, not the box next to the link), they'll be taken to a page that displays 25 other books sharing the same tag. By default these books are ranked by "Recently Popular" which actually means "**Recently downloaded a lot!**"

The reason I said "**recently downloaded**" and not "sold" is because I see a book on this list that has a price of $0. So if you get a lot of free downloads when you run a free promo day, then you could show up on the first page for certain tags.

This list can also be sorted by <u>recently added</u>, <u>recently tagged</u>, and <u>popularity</u>. If you add a new book to Amazon, then your book will show up for that specific tag when you sort by **recently added**. You can also contact your friends or family and ask them to click the tags on your book. That will help your book show up when sorted by **recently tagged**.

Don't forget to use your email list too! Even if you only have 10-20 email subscribers, that's okay! You can set up an auto responder asking your subscribers to review your book one week, then click your "Like" button another week, and finally to **click your tags**.

Should You Create Multiple Pen-Names?
About a month ago, my sister was searching on Amazon for cookbooks. She found a cookbook that she wanted to buy, but she decided to click on the authors "Author Central" link first. When she looked through the author's books, she noticed **cookbooks**, **sex books**, **marketing books**, and some books about **dreams**.

She was <u>confused</u> so she called me over to her computer. She thought she clicked on the wrong screen and she was trying to figure out how to get back to the cookbooks. I showed her how to get back to the cookbooks, and I left to finish what I was doing.

I talked to her later that day, and it turns out that she purchased **a completely different book** from a different author. When I asked her why, she said because she wanted to buy a book from someone that <u>really knows</u> about cooking recipes.

So I learned that if you're a non-fiction author, you need to keep your books organized. If you decide to write cookbooks, then you should **use a specific pen-name** for all your cookbooks. If you want to write sex books, then **use a different pen-name** for those books too. You can keep the publishers name the same, but just change the author's name.

The Amazon community isn't filled with idiots. These people read books for fun, so they're more educated than your average couch potato that watches TV all day. So if you write books on 20 different subjects and list them under the same pen-name, a consumer (like my sister) <u>might not take you serious</u> and look for another book.

If another author see's that you have 20 books on 20 different subjects, then we're not going to take you serious either. You'll come off as one of those guys that purchased a **"Make Money with Amazon Kindle"** starter kit, and now you're pumping out 99 cents books that you probably didn't even write. Do you really want to be known as that guy?

There's nothing wrong with publishing books on Amazon just to make money, but **you need to be professional** about it. Imagine if you clicked on Stephen King's author central profile, and you saw a random cookbook for $2.99. You'd probably think you clicked on the wrong page too like my sister did.

This is mainly a problem with indie non-fiction authors. I hardly ever see this problem with fiction authors because they usually stay in the same book genre.

Chapter 10

Bonus Tips

As you sell more books, you'll start to climb the best sellers rank within your specific category. If you get on the bestsellers list and consistently stay there, then update your book cover with a "Bestseller" logo.

You can find a lot of professional "Bestseller" logos from http://shutterstock.com. A bestseller logo is **social proof** that a lot of people are buying your book which will help you sell more books. People like to buy bestselling books just because everybody else is buying it.

You can purchase a good logo for under $20. If you don't have the extra cash, then you can use Google to find free "royalty free" logos that you can use. You can add the logo to the book yourself using Photoshop, or pay *Access Ideas* www.elance.com/s/accessideas (The freelancers from Elance.com) to update your book cover for you. They shouldn't charge you more than $10.

Link Your Books Together

If you have more than one book on Amazon, then you should link your books together. At the end of your books, you should add a page that says something like "**More Books From This Author**." On that page you can add the title to your other books, the Amazon link, and a picture of your book too.

I think it's very important to add a picture of the book so people can see what it looks like. If people start to see your book enough times, they'll eventually buy it to see what the hype is all about. They'll think it's a popular book, and everybody wants to own the popular book. (i.e Bestsellers.)

Remember to **only link related books** together. Don't link your "*Sci-Fi Horror*" book to your "*Lose 10lbs in 10 Days*" book. I already discussed this earlier, so I'm not going to go into that again.

KDP Select Free Promo Tips

You should only run your free promo days for **24 hours** at a time. It's a bad idea to run a free promotion for 5 days in a row because you only get 5 free days within a 90 day period.

You're going to need those free days to help with your "Verified Purchase Reviews" which you'll need to coordinate. To run your free promo for 24 hours, make sure to select the *start date* and the *end date* as the same day. (*Figure 82.*)

Figure 82

If your book sells start to fall off, you can <u>run a free day to boost your sales</u>. If you recall, your book will move up the "Top Free List" when people download it for free. As your book starts to move up the list, a lot more people will see your book and download it. If your new readers like your book, then they'll recommend it to their friends and buy other books that you've written.

<u>**Most Important:**</u> When your free promo ends, your book will show up on a related bestsellers product page in the section that says "**Customers Who Bought This Item Also Bought**." Even though people didn't actually buy your book, it'll still show up in that section if you received a lot of free downloads.

Press Release Websites

An online press release can sometimes help you **shut out the competition**. If you decide to use an online press release company, you should choose a company that's more likely to get you included in "Google News." Here's a list of six press release websites worth checking out. Some are free, some are paid, and some are both free and paid:

1. www.pressmethod.com
2. www.free-press-release-center.info
3. www.sbwire.com
4. www.pr.com
5. www.i-newswire.com
6. www.prweb.com

The United Kingdom

Amazon has a completely different website for people in the United Kingdom. The website can be found by visiting: **http://www.amazon.co.uk/**

If you're a self published author, then there's a 90% chance that you don't have any book reviews on the UK website. So if you want to sell more books, make sure that you try to get book reviews in the UK too. You can find people easily with a simple Google search and/or outsourcing websites.

You can have readers in the UK download your book while you're running a FREE promo campaign. If you run out of free promo days, then you can ask them to purchase the book and then just reimburse them via Papal. I don't recommend using the Amazon "gift" feature because you have to buy your own book to "gift" it, and it won't show up as a verified purchase review.

Amazon also has a separate "Author Central" for the United Kingdom. The website can be found at: **https://authorcentral.amazon.co.uk/**

Simply copy everything from your U.S. Author Central account, and paste it to the UK website. This should only take you about 15 minutes, and it's worth the effort. A lot of self published authors don't optimize their books for the United Kingdom. I've found that most authors either don't know about the UK website, or they add it to their "to-do list" and never do it.

Change Book Cover & Title

If your book sales are horrible, don't be afraid to change the title of the book cover. If you recall earlier, I suggested that you come up with a few different book titles and choose the best one. Well maybe you didn't choose the best title, so try a different one and see if your sales improve.

You can also change the image or color on your book cover. I used a different shade of "blue" on one of my books, and my sales literally sky rocketed. That's the beauty of Amazon Kindle Publishing. You can make changes anytime you want, and just upload the new files.

If you decide to change the image on your book cover, I recommend that you purchase an image that's at least 300dpi (dots per inch.) If you decide to create a paperback book in the future, then you'll need a 300dpi high resolution image. So it's better to buy this image from the start so you don't have to buy the same image again later.

From personal experience, I purchased a low resolution image for my first book. The image only cost me about $30. When I decided to create a paperback book, the freelancer informed me that the image needed to be at least 300dpi. So I went to re-purchase the image, and guess what? The same image in 300dpi format was $275! There was no way that I was going to pay that much for one image, so I had to change my entire book cover.

So learn from my experience and just buy the high resolution image from the beginning. There are thousands of 300dpi images available for $20-$30. This will enable you to use that same image for your kindle book and your paperback book.

Create Paperback Books
If you want to create a paperback book, Amazon has a print on demand division called "CreateSpace." You can visit their website at: **https://www.createspace.com**.

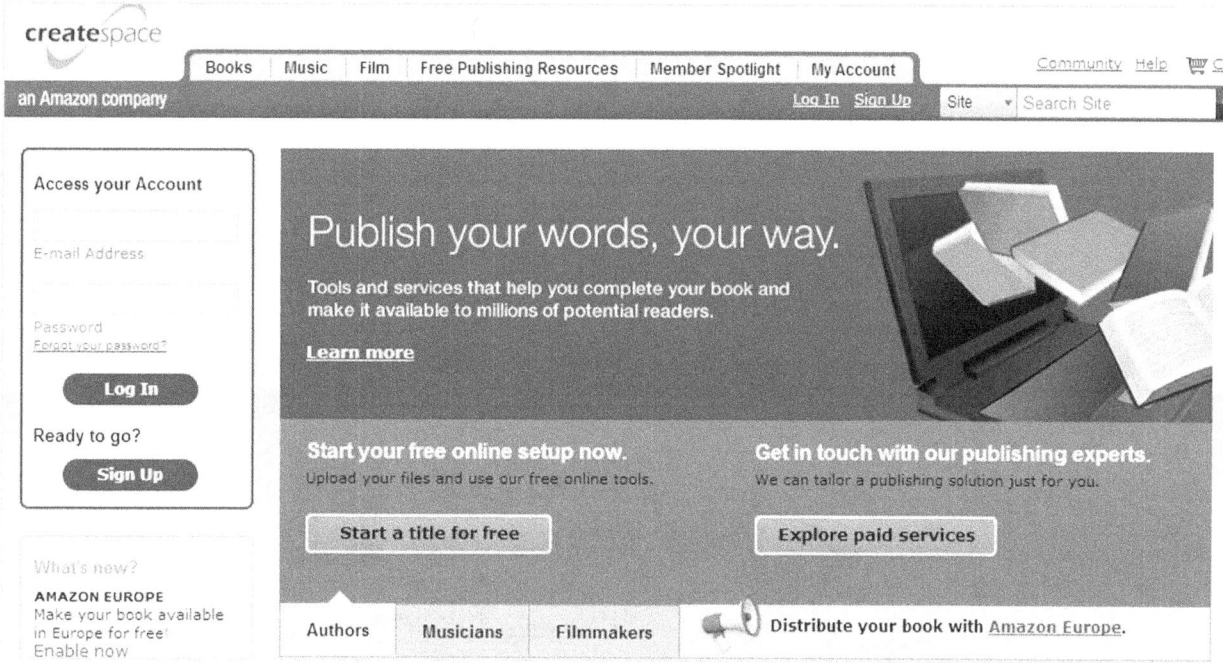

You can hire *Access Ideas* www.elance.com/s/accessideas (Elance outsourcing company) to format your book for CreateSpace. I've also heard that some people have used **Fivver.com** to get their books formatted for Createspace. All the "gigs" on Fiverr only cost $5. If you're on a really tight budget then you can experiment with Fiverr to see what happens.

The CreateSpace process is very similar to the Kindle publishing process. The only major differences is that you get to choose if your book is in color of black & white, size of your book, and you need an ISBN (International Standard Book Number.) Amazon will give you an ISBN for free, so you don't have to worry about that part. For more details, visit their website.

More Distribution Options

If you'd like to distribute your book to the *Apple iBookstore*, *Barnes & Noble*, *Sony*, *Kobo*, *Baker & Taylor*, and *Diesel*, then you should publish your book with Smashwords as well. You can visit their website by using this link: **http://www.smashwords.com**.

How to Create, Publish and Distribute Ebooks with Smashwords

Once again, you can hire *Access Ideas* www.elance.com/s/accessideas to format your book for Smashwords if you'd like. When you publish your book to Smashwords, they will distribute your book to all the major retailers listed above.

It's important to note that Smashwords pays your royalties quarterly. So you will only get paid 4 times per year with Smashwords compared to every month with Amazon. If you decide to publish with Smashwords, then you can't enroll your book into Amazon's KDP Select program.

When you choose to enroll your book in KDP Select, you're committing to make the digital format of that book available exclusively through Kindle Direct Publishing. During the period of exclusivity, you cannot distribute your book digitally anywhere else, including on your website, blogs, etc. However, you can continue to distribute your book in physical format, or in any format other than digital.

For more information, you can visit this link: **https://kdp.amazon.com/self-publishing/KDPSelect**

Audio books

Depending on your book genre, you might want to create an audio book. Some people like to listen to books on CD while they're driving around town. You can also sell audio books for double the price of your paperback book.

You can record the audio yourself, or pay a freelancer (search Elance.com) to perform this task for you. People like to consume information in different ways. The more avenues you provide, the more readers you'll reach.

Rebecca V.

Audiobook narrator, voice over talent

United States | Design & Multimedia _3_ | 1 Jobs | $110 Earnings | ✰✰✰✰✰

I am an experienced audiobook narrator and voice over talent with numerous titles to my name and lots of very happy and satisfied customers. I have trained with one of the all-time top audiobook...

▶ Portfolio | Skills: Audiobook narration, audiobook production, voice over, singing

Social Bookmarking & Social Media

You can use social bookmarking websites to drive web traffic to your product page. Some social bookmarking websites are:

- Stumbleupon.com
- Delicious.com
- Digg.com
- Reddit.com

I recommend that you social bookmark all of your product pages, your author central profiles, and your review pages. If you're short on time, then you can also outsource this task using websites like:

- Fiverr.com
- Elance.com
- Microworkers.com

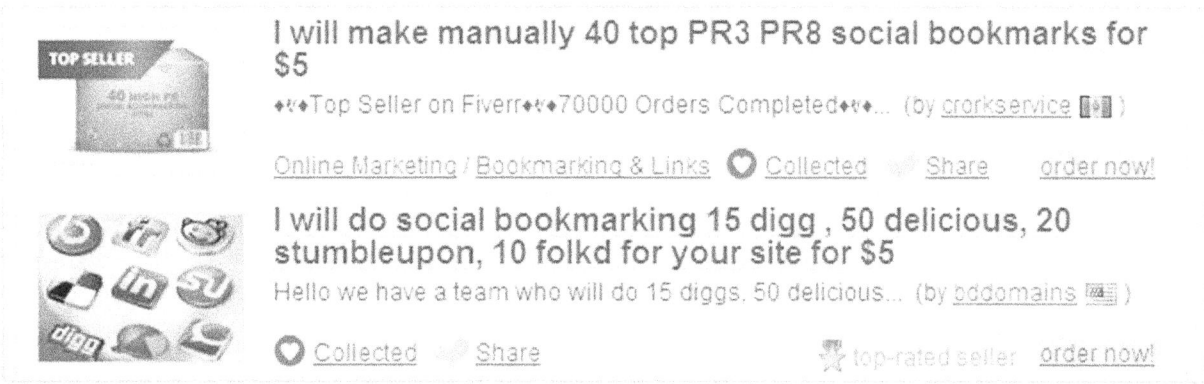

I will make manually 40 top PR3 PR8 social bookmarks for $5

♦ᵥ♦Top Seller on Fiverr♦ᵥ♦70000 Orders Completed♦ᵥ♦... (by crorkservice)

Online Marketing / Bookmarking & Links ○ Collected ◇ Share   order now!

I will do social bookmarking 15 digg , 50 delicious, 20 stumbleupon, 10 folkd for your site for $5

Hello we have a team who will do 15 diggs, 50 delicious... (by oddomains)

○ Collected ◇ Share   ☆ top-rated seller order now!

You should also syndicate your book to Facebook and Twitter, but I recommend that you outsource this task too. You don't want to self-promote yourself too much on social networks. It's 100% better if you hire other people do this for you because it will seem natural.

Even if your sales still seem slow, continue to use Social Bookmarking and Social Media. You want people to see your book everywhere they turn. The more they see your book; the more likely they are to buy it because it will become familiar to them.

Remember *"The Rule of Seven."* It says that a prospect needs to see or hear your marketing message at least seven times before they take action and buy from you.

So make sure that your syndicate your book to websites that get a lot of traffic. If you'd like to get a list of websites that get the most traffic in the world, then visit this link: **http://www.alexa.com/topsites**.

Conclusion

None of the information in this eBook is *guaranteed* to increase your sales. I've seen useless books move into Amazons Top 100 paid; and there are some amazing books that barely sell a few copies per month.

There's **NO TOP SECRET** trick to that will help you become a New York Times Bestseller. No matter what you do, you can't force people to buy your book. Just try your best to get your pen-name out there, and give your book(s) as much **exposure** as possible.

If you write an amazing book, then people will buy it and spread the word about you. If your book doesn't sell that well, then make a few changes to your book cover and title and try again.

The truth is that <u>nobody really knows</u> why one books sells and an equally good book doesn't. Just don't give up and keep writing. You're probably a lot closer to reaching your goals than you think.

-Kent Mauresmo & Anastasiya Petrova

<u>www.Read2Learn.net</u>

Get the PDF version of this Book

To download the full color PDF version of this book,
visit the link below:
http://read2learn.net/54321-2/

More Business Training Books by Read2Learn:

"How To Build a Website With WordPress...Fast! [2nd Edition]"
Buy this book now on Amazon!

"SEO For WordPress (Beginners Guide)"
Get This Book Now on Amazon!

www.ingramcontent.com/pod-product-compliance
Lightning Source LLC
Chambersburg PA
CBHW081139170526
45165CB00008B/2736